SUPERNATURAL

SUPERNATURAL

Reb Buxton

Supernatural:
an event beyond scientific explanation or defies the laws of nature

I see things behind things behind things
There are rings within rings within rings

Things Behind Things Behind Things
Bon Iver

There is not a code to the heavenly vault that God is waiting on you to learn so you can unlock the spiritual gifts you don't currently have. There is only a still small whisper and learning more and more to detect it and say yes to it in our everyday lives.

Tyler Staton

Do you believe in miracles?

Ted Lasso

(c)2025 Reb Buxton
All Rights Reserved

SUPERNATURAL
Evidence For Miracles In Everyday Life

No part of this book may be reproduced in any form or by any electronic or mechanical means, including information storage and retrieval systems, without permission in writing from the author, except by reviewers, who may quote brief passages in a review.

ISBN 978-1-7323788-7-2

Design and illustrations by Reb Buxton, M.A., O.S.B.
Printed in the United States of America
Published by The Flow Farm Press
Nashville, TN

Visit the author's website at www.rebbuxton.com

Contents

1	TRANSFORMATION	7
2	MIRACLES, SIGNS, & WONDERS	9
3	A PRAYER TO A SILENT GOD	16
4	THE MIRACLE OF THE SUNGLASSES	20
5	THE MIRACLE OF JOY	28
6	THE MIRACLE ON THE GREENWAY	44
7	THE MIRACLE OF THE NOTE FROM GOD	55
8	THE MIRACLE OF NOT GOING	67
9	THE MIRACLE OF THE BULLET & SIPPY CUP	77
10	THE MIRACLE OF THE PEACOCK	93
11	THE MIRACLE OF THE TRASHCAN	100
12	THE MIRACLE OF TIMING	108
13	THE MIRACLE OF IMAGINATION	117
14	WAITING ON A MIRACLE	152
15	PRAYING FOR A MIRACLE	155

About the Author   157

1

TRANSFORMATION

It was neither psychological theories nor theological doctrines that ultimately rescued me from myself, my past, my wounds, and my self-sabotaging behaviors. What transformed me were actual healing experiences. When I have experienced love from another person, it has healed me. When I have experienced the love of God in the form of a miracle, it has healed me. Knowledge is necessary but never sufficient. What you know in your mind must be experienced in your real life and real relationships; otherwise, it will remain just an idea, powerless and pregnant with possibility. Ideas inform, but it is our experiences that transform.

Transformation is often used in a positive context but it is a neutral word. Traumatic experiences transform us in one way. Healing experiences transform us in another. Unfortunately, we have all had too many negative experiences that have wounded us. If we truly want healing, we must create more positive experiences that counter the negative, wounding experiences.

Talk therapy and prayer are two common paths Westerners use to solve problems and heal their emotional wounds. However, if these practices do not lead to experiences that open up one's heart, mind, body, and soul to change, growth, courage, compassion, and love they are ultimately powerless. This isn't to say that therapy and prayer have no purpose, they do, but they are modes of transportation to move you toward healing experiences, not an end in and of themselves.

When it comes to the difference between knowledge and experience, I will let the haunting words from an anonymous Rwandan genocide survivor speak to the cavernous gap between the two:

> *We had a lot of trouble with Western mental health workers who came here immediately after the genocide, and we had to ask them to leave. They came and their practice did not involve being outside in the sun where you began to feel better. There was no music or drumming to get your blood flowing again. There was no sense that everyone had taken the day off so that the entire community could come together to try to lift you up and bring you back to joy. There was no acknowledgment of the depression as something invasive, and external that could actually be cast out again. Instead, they would take one at a time into these dingy, little rooms and have them sit around for an hour or so and talk about bad things that happened to them. We had to ask them to leave.*

2

MIRACLES, SIGNS, & WONDERS

Do miracles, signs, and wonders still happen today like they did in biblical times? Is there an unseen realm at work around us arranging miraculous experiences? Can we do anything to bring more miracles into our lives? The short answer to all these questions is yes!

As I pondered writing a book about miracles I talked with clergy and lay people about the subject. What I found is that everyone has strong opinions about the word miracle.

Many people shy away from using the word miracle to describe an event in their everyday lives, wanting to reserve it as a more reverential term to describe epic feats such as Jesus healing a blind man or the parting of the Red Sea. The consensus seemed to be that signs and wonders are impressive but of a lesser rank than a bona fide miracle and should be treated as such. They are probably right but I am no theologian. So, for the sake of brevity, I chose to use the word miracle to include both signs and wonders.

A general definition of a miracle is a divinely orchestrated event. This idea can be subdivided into more specific categories. One type of miracle that consistently appears in the following stories are ordinary events with extraordinary timing that have a deep personal meaning. Nearly all of the stories in this book involve ordinary events. However, when it comes to miraculous events, it is the timing that appears supernatural.

This may seem obvious, but I don't believe we have the ability to summon a miracle through our own efforts. What we can do is make ourselves more sensitive to the presence of miracles by living in ways that pry open our often guarded and fearful hearts.

I do not believe it is necessary to be a Christian to receive the gift of a miracle. God loves us all, not just those who ascribe to a certain religion. We are all made in the image of God and are worthy of dignity and respect. Whether Christian, of another faith, atheist, or agnostic, every miracle points to God, not us. Our only job in the mysterious event is to receive it as a gift.

But let's be real for a moment. You are not reading this book to learn more about me. It's okay. I'm not offended. You are here for you. Anyone interested in reading a book titled *SUPERNATURAL* is for sure looking for their own wild experiences, not just to read about someone else's. If you just wanted to be entertained with a good story, it would be much easier to turn on Netflix than to read a book.

The truth is we all want more miracles in our lives because we all have impossible problems that could use a healthy dose of divine intervention. There is a little part in all of us that wants to believe in magic, in something greater than ourselves, in a cosmic battle of good against evil, a benevolent universe, a supernatural world we cannot see. We desperately hope we are not stuck here alone on this rock hurling through a lifeless void to be met with infinite darkness at the moment of death. This is why we go to church. This is why we watch TV shows like *Stranger Things* and movies like *Star Wars*. This is why we read books with the word "miracles" in the subtitle.

If there is one thing I am certain of it is this: Any sincere seeker of truth, love, hope, wisdom, courage, peace, and integrity will find God and be shown miraculous experiences. Why? Not because they earned them but because this type of living animates the heart and mind to the threads of serendipity at work all around. This is of utmost importance to grasp if you want to catch a glimpse of the supernatural world at work. You will miss so much if you are lost in the muck and mire of poor decisions and pessimistic thinking. Instead of finding miracles, you will self-sabotage.

How do I know this is true? Because I have lived both lives. I have lived in ways that have caused me great loss and hurt those I love. I was blind, wandering around lost in my own life. I exemplified what Jesus called with great contempt, a whitewashed tomb kind of life. I was a hypocrite and I didn't even recognize it.

I now seek to live each day with love, wisdom, and integrity and I encourage you to do the same. One of the great gifts of living in this way is a deep sense of peace. I now have peace. I am at peace. I share this peace with others.

Before jumping into the miracles, here are a few assumptions made:

1. God exists. God is love. God loves you.
2. Evil is real. It is your enemy. It is intelligent. It wants to destroy you.
3. There is a supernatural realm we cannot see where divine beings are at work on our behalf to accomplish the will of God through us and for us.
4. We are *all* created in the image of God and thereby worthy of dignity and respect.
5. There is one God. All sincere seekers of the divine are searching for the one true God no matter what they call

him. It is up to God to examine the hearts of every person.
6. When it comes to spirituality, it is my job to worry about my side of the street, not sit in judgment of anyone's spiritual experience.
7. Many people who call themselves Christians are what Jesus called whitewashed tombs. His analogy was to newly painted burial sites that looked nice on the outside but inside were full of disease and death. I am not contradicting assumption #6. This is an observation not a judgment. I have great compassion for anyone stuck in hypocrisy and I want to help! It is a path that leads to death in so many ways. I know this to be true because I used to be a whitewashed tomb kinda guy.
8. Miracles, signs, and wonders are real. They happen all around us. You do not need to be a Christian or of any faith to receive miracles from God because they are graces given not tokens earned for good deeds done.
9. In regards to witnessing more miracles, you can only make yourself more sensitive to see the miracles as they happen. There is a joy in being able to witness the unfolding drama of a divine gift. Seeing the extraordinary in the ordinary moments of everyday life will boost your faith.
10. There will never be enough miracles to satisfy the human heart. Miracles only satisfy for a time until the memory of the experience fades and our restless hearts long for more. Every miracle does offer a special memory to carry as a gift, giving our hearts something to cling to when life gets difficult.

Each story in this book is like an episode of a TV show. Some episodes are funny while others are dark and dramatic. No matter the tone of a specific episode, each one moves the story closer to the dramatic conclusion that indeed there is an unseen realm at work on your behalf.

As I wrote each chapter several common threads began to emerge.

Providential Timing - When the timing of an event is beyond something that could have been arranged by human means or defies explanation, you are likely in the midst of a divinely orchestrated event. Embrace the moment! Cherish it! *The Miracle of the Sunglasses* and *The Miracle of Timing* are good examples of this.

Freewill To Choose - Without fail, every story contains critical moments when an important choice needed to be made that allowed for either a beautiful moment to emerge or to prevent something bad from happening. At the time they are happening, these critical moments often seem unremarkable.

Warnings - *The Bullet in the Sippy Cup* may be the most dramatic example of the dire consequences that can occur when obvious warning signs are blatantly ignored.

Call To Change/Take Action - *The Miracle on the Greenway* is the most profound example of receiving a message that called me to live with a greater, higher purpose.

Life-Changing Information - There were two messages in particular that forever altered the course of my life. The first was to live each day with love, wisdom, and integrity and the second was the call to live a more formal religious life.

Manifestation of Spiritual Gifts in the Physical World - God writing me a note and finding the sunglasses are examples of the supernatural breaking through to the physical realm.

Ideas Of Unknown Origin - Every divine message I have heard over the years did not appear to originate from my own thinking. Rather, they felt as if they came from some external source. I had not been thinking about the virtues of love, wisdom, and integrity prior to that thought coming to mind. It felt strange and unfamiliar. The same is true for the directive to live a more formal religious life. That in no way felt like a thought I conjured on my own. Each revelation left me with a sense of surprise and a, "Where did that come from?" feeling.

Chaos Follows Disobedience - My priest once said to me, "All sin has consequences". The story of my attempted murder and the experience in Yellowstone National Park are poignant examples of the chaos surrounding disobedience to divine wisdom and going my own way.

Anything Can Be Used In Service Of A Miracle - Sunglasses in a pile of trash, a note found in the woods, a gaggle of laughing monks, a filthy garbage can, an email. These and more were used to bring spiritual messages to me.

The Power of Prayer - I do not claim to understand how prayer works or why it works sometimes and not others. I only know it has played an integral role in my spiritual life and these miraculous experiences. *The Miracle of the Note from God* is a perfect example of prayer appearing to influence a response.

Humility - In each case, there was a moment when I needed a dose of humility to move forward. *The Miracle of the Trashcan* serves as a prime example of a moment when my ego could have gotten out of hand had I not made the choice years ago to live with love, wisdom, and integrity. As a result of choosing humility, I was given the gift of preventing a major problem from occurring.

Supernatural Intervention To Stop A Tragedy - *The Miracle of Timing* is a great example of a divine intervention. With every miracle that happened that day, there was still a man who chose to drive while on drugs that died a fiery death and nearly killed a mother and her kids in the process. This story epitomizes the struggle between darkness and light.

Use Of The Body For Spiritual Messages - In the story *The Miracle of Not Going* I share how I was overcome with a deep depression on the eve of leaving for graduate school. This was an overwhelming physical sensation I could not ignore. While it felt terrible, it worked well to get my attention. In retrospect, I see it as a divine gift that helped me focus and get the clarity I needed. As soon as I made the decision not to go, the depression lifted.

I now live expecting miracles to happen. I find this a hopeful way to live. As Albert Einstein reminds us, "There are two ways to live your life. One is as though nothing is a miracle. The other is as though everything is a miracle."

3

A PRAYER TO A SILENT GOD

Something inside of me halts every time I attempt to write or say the words, "God spoke to me," or "God told me." Many infamous people throughout history have claimed the same moral high ground to justify terrible acts. My halting response is an attempt to protect myself from being associated with that crazy crowd. Yet, here I am about to proclaim a book full of God told me's.

If I am being honest I don't know who or what is sending me these messages and experiences. I only know that I have had enough of them to believe they are authentic. I only assume they are from God because I don't have another bucket to put them in. Another telltale sign that these messages have a divine origin are the positive outcomes that follow.

In the summer of 2024, I heard the familiar voice I attribute to God. The message was that it was time for me to "live a more formal religious life". What was so strange about this message was that I had not been to church in more than five years.

Before my divorce, my family attended St. Bartholomew's Episcopal Church from 2003-2019. By early 2020 our divorce was in full swing, the Episcopal church was spasming over the issue of gay clergy, the longtime priest we adored retired, and the global killing machine known as the COVID-19 pandemic was just ramping up. It felt like the appropriate time to retreat from the world.

While I was somewhat confused about what it meant to live a more formal religious life, I took the directive seriously. I go into greater detail about how this played itself out in the chapter *The Miracle Of Imagination.*

Soon after receiving the directive, a friend suggested I listen to a podcast called *Turning To The Mystics.* Every season featured a different Christian mystic. I have always admired and drawn inspiration from Thomas Merton so that is where I chose to begin listening.

Jim Finley is the host of the podcast. He and Merton were both monks at the Abbey of Gethsemani at the same time. On the podcast, he discusses the life and works of Merton in great detail offering insightful anecdotes about his interactions with Merton.

In one episode Finley reads *The Merton Prayer,* as it has come to be known, and it inspired me to write a prayer of my own. I felt the need to express both my struggle and desire to connect with God.

One of the first prayers I wrote was about the problem of the silence of God. It is called *Be Still - A Prayer To A Silent God.* I acknowledge the irony of beginning a book about hearing from God with a prayer about the silence of God. I can only say that my life has been filled with far more silence, often long years of painful silence, than divine messages so this seems an appropriate topic to address at the start of our journey together.

As we contemplate the idea of miracles, I want to begin with reverential gratitude for you. Thank you for being here reading these words, whoever you are, wherever you may be, and whatever you may be going through. I am praying for you.

BE STILL - A Prayer To A Silent God

God,

Despite what I may think or feel at any moment, I am not certain of what it is I need or what you want from me. And when I do ask for what I think I want or need, my prayers often go unanswered. This leads me to conclude that either I am far adrift from your divine will for my life or your silence is essential to our relationship. While this can often feel lonely, I do not feel left alone by you.

I am striving to let go of how I want you to be and accept how and when you choose to reveal yourself. In this, I am seeking to free my mind of so many misguided beliefs about you.

So often my requests, no matter how sincere, seem to make little difference to the outcome of a situation and only weaken my faith in your goodness and sow seeds of disappointment in my heart. As a result, I have become exhausted with talking prayers. I love you and I trust that you know what I need even before I ask. Because you know me and what I need better than I do, I will meet your silence with my own reverential silence. In this silence, I will seek to be with you, not seek anything from you.

I ask forgiveness for attempting to make you into my image so you might do my bidding. I choose to trust that when you make your invisible presence known, it will be both good and timely. If you allow something I love to be taken, the reason will most likely remain hidden in your quietude, and therefore would be foolish to seek any explanation. This is not the God I want but rather the God of my experience and that of countless millions both now and throughout history.

May you correct where I am wrong and reveal to me your Truth. I release all superstitious illusions that if I say a certain prayer, at a certain time, do good deeds to gain your favor, or continually and earnestly repeat my requests you will somehow be persuaded to bend to my will and answer my prayers. No more sacrilege. No more begging for miracles. No more. No more. No more. I am free. I am free. At last, I am free.

4

THE MIRACLE OF THE SUNGLASSES

This is a parable. This is also a true story.

There once was a man who owned a pair of sunglasses for many years. He liked the sunglasses because they made him look handsome and protected his aging eyes from the sun.

Over the years the glasses fell into disrepair. He made the trek through the green hills back to the hut where he bought the sunglasses. The glassworkers happily repaired and polished them to look as good as new.

One day the man found his sunglasses needed yet another repair. He returned to the hut where a somber glassworker relayed the news that there was nothing more they could do. One of the small holes that connected the lenses to the arm was stripped and beyond repair. The man left disappointed but not discouraged. In no time at all he found a solution.

The man found his fishing pole and cut a small piece of fishing line. He connected the arm to the sunglasses threading the fishing line through the now stripped hole where the tiny screw once lived. Using overhand knots the man quickly repaired the glasses.

For quite a long time this worked. When the fishing line failed with all the folding and bending, the man cut another piece and tied it all back together once again.

The sunglasses developed another problem. If they were laid down too hard or fell from the man's hands to the ground, as sunglasses are apt to do, the left lens would pop out like a kernel of corn in a pot full of hot oil. The man was annoyed when this happened but as he had grown more fond of his ragtag pair of sunglasses he found a way to pop the lens back in and keep on with life.

Then one fateful day the sunglasses met their untimely end.

One evening while the man was picking up his daughter he forgot he had placed the sunglasses in the passenger's seat. It was nighttime and the man's daughter didn't see them. Without realizing it the daughter sat on the glasses, smashing and bending them terribly. The man did not realize this until the next day. He was sad but worked to see if he could somehow bend the frame back into a somewhat wearable shape. He could and he did! The sunglasses lived to see another day!

Some weeks later the man mindlessly placed the sunglasses back in the passenger seat. Then one day after a meeting, he took a friend home. Again, it was dark and the man forgot about his sunglasses. His friend innocently sat on the sunglasses crushing them once again. This time there would be no repair. The man was heartbroken but knew he needed another pair to protect his eyes.

The man went back to the hut and found the perfect pair of sunglasses. There was only one problem, they cost $295. The man knew that he would have them for years but did not think it wise to spend $300 on a pair of sunglasses.

The man searched other stores, looked online, and even went to the big box retailers hoping to find a somewhat reasonably priced pair of similar glasses. The man did not have any luck.

Day and night the man wrestled with what to do. Finally, he concluded it was not wise to spend so much money on a pair of glasses and decided to go without. Then something strange happened...

The man loved to run both for exercise and for pleasure. He ran in the heat and he ran in the cold. He ran when it was wet and when it was dry.

One day at the end of a run the man slowed to a walk to cool down. It was common for the man to walk with his head down because he often pondered deep thoughts and staring down at the ground encouraged contemplation and minimized distractions.

On this day as he walked beneath an underpass, he looked down to see a pile of rubbish filled with rocks, sand, and garbage. This was a common sight on this section of road because it was a place where the unhoused congregated and stormwater pooled collecting silt and garbage.

As the man passed by the trash, something caught his eye. It looked like a small box. The man continued walking but was stopped by a thought urging him to go back and investigate the little box in the pile of trash. So he did.

The man looked around to see if anyone was watching. He felt embarrassed that someone he knew might catch him scrounging through the trash but he did it anyway and found the box. The small box looked very much like a sunglasses case. The man knelt down to get a better look. He picked up the little box and opened it. Inside was a pair of sunglasses, "No way! You've got to be kidding me!" the man said, wonder-struck.

The man took the sunglasses home and cleaned them. They were a perfectly fine pair of sunglasses and his girlfriend loved them!

The man noticed on the arm of the sunglasses the name TOM FORD. Out of curiosity and not recognizing the brand the man searched online for the sunglasses. Within a few minutes, he found the exact pair. and the price . . . $285.

The man laughed. He had found his new pair of sunglasses or better said they found him!

The sunglasses on top were the old Ray Bans. The glasses on the bottom are the "new" Tom Ford glasses found beneath the overpass.

The tunnel where the Tom Ford sunglasses were found.

SO WHAT?

Why should this matter to you?

At first glance, it's just a quirky anecdote—me wanting a pair of sunglasses and stumbling upon them, improbably, under a bridge in a pile of trash. But it's exactly this kind of moment that makes one stop and wonder: *Is something bigger at work here?*

This wasn't a life and death situation. It was small, personal, and seemingly insignificant—and that's the point. It reveals something deeply comforting: God cares, even about the little things. The sunglasses were never the miracle. The miracle was the reminder that my needs are seen, heard, and known.

So what? Well, that changes things. It tells me the divine presence doesn't just show up in burning bushes or in the parting of seas—it shows up in the pausing, the restraint, in the decision *not* to spend $300 I didn't have. And it shows up under bridges, in garbage piles, and in the quiet when you listen instead of rushing through the day.

You can't manufacture moments like these. You can't force miracles by being good or by trying harder. Miracles aren't rewards for good behavior. They're interruptions of grace and being open to them requires not perfection, but attention.

So what *is* required of us? Stillness. Humility. Listening. Living with spiritual curiosity. Being willing to trust that God is not only real but good—and good to *you*. That kind of faith doesn't just believe; it waits and it anchors itself in community, prayer, and discernment.

And when the miraculous breaks through—even in something as mundane as finding sunglasses—don't keep it to yourself. Share it. Because others need to know what we so easily forget: the veil between heaven and earth is thinner than we think. And sometimes, heaven shows up right in the mess of our everyday lives.

5

THE MIRACLE OF JOY

The section of highway connecting Nashville, Tennessee to St. Meinrad's monastery begins in a teeming metropolis full of construction cranes and endless traffic and ends on a quiet dead-end road in southern Indiana just north of the small township of Santa Claus. It was on a particularly vibrant October day that I found myself in this secluded monastery seeking quiet refuge from a busy life and a little guidance from a monk. I found both and a whole lot more.

The majestic cathedral of the archabbey is the centerpiece of life at the monastery. It is where the monks gather to pray, sing, and live out the ceremonies of monastic life five times each day.

The architecture of the magnificent structure was formed from large, hand-cut sandstone blocks dragged by mules and horses from the nearby quarry a few miles away starting in 1899. Each stone block weighs more than 800 pounds. The steps leading up to the triptych of red doors are made from pure white Tennessee marble.

Three marble statues of saints sit atop each door keeping watchful eyes over all who enter. In the center is the Madonna and Child known as Our Lady of Einsiedeln. On the Madonna's right is St. Benedict who wrote *The Rule of St. Benedict* in the sixth century as a guide for how to run a monastery and live the monastic life. This rule is still followed today by Benedictine monks worldwide. To the left of Mary, Mother of Jesus, is St. Scholastica, the twin sister of St. Benedict.

Inside the church, the hard right angles of the granite floors and sandstone walls hold aloft the picturesque domed ceilings painted with majestic frescoes of biblical dramas. The stone floors and concrete columns shape the cathedral into a large cross.

As the monks begin chanting their prayers, the atmosphere transforms, vibrating with life, filling the majestic cathedral with ethereal harmonies that are otherworldly.

There may be no better place to enter the silence of God than a monastery. The quiet permeates every square foot of land, every human, and every building. Even when the silence is broken with conversation or laughter, there is always a riptide pulling one back out into the deep waters of reverential silence.

The landscape is peppered with hidden trails and quiet gardens that encourage silence and reflection. There are two lakes with walking paths leading into the pine forest where hidden shrines bring delight at their surprise discovery. Here, nature's simple, ever-evolving beauty ushers in a sacred silence not different from the cathedral but requiring no architect or stonemason.

Being so far away from urban lights and sounds, the night is darker than dark, and the quiet more quiet than a graveyard. This is a rare kind of silence. The shadow side of this tranquility is that any soul not at peace will find the quiet solitude amplifying their inner turmoil. Silence to someone racked with guilt or who is in the throws of a tumultuous season may quickly devolve into fear-soaked suffering. Without the love of God to guide and protect in such a hostile inner landscape, the silence does not feel like a safe place. With the support of the Spirit of Truth, rest is possible even in the midst of great personal upheaval. This is why so many hungry souls seek out the solitude of monasteries.

Up a small hill, a stone's throw away from the cathedral is the guesthouse. This is where visitors and groups stay during retreats. There are comfortable rooms, a front desk, a relaxing lobby full of floating rocking chairs and books, meeting rooms, a small chapel, offices, and a cafeteria that is open 24 hours a day. It was in one of the offices that I found myself with Father Eugene excited about my first spiritual direction session with a bona fide monk.

I immediately felt at peace in his presence. I am a collector of sorts when it comes to inner peace. I seek out people, places, and experiences that foster an inner calm and a peaceful heart, mind, and body. So many people find it difficult to feel at peace. This simple, free gift escapes them. This is a quiet tragedy full of silent suffering.

Father Eugene's office was warmly lit and modestly appointed with comfortable chairs and a bookshelf full of wisdom. The only out-of-place oddity was a four-foot-tall replica of King Tut's sarcophagus standing upright with a straw hat on top.

When I first entered, Father Eugune greeted me at the door with a nondescript expression. He was neither effusive nor cold and seemed to be a man of immense practicality and matter-of-factness common to farmers and those from the Midwest. His eyes were discerning and his long, solid white beard rounded at the bottom formed a half-haloed hairy nimbus that accentuated his piercing eyes and mystical presence.

The black hooded habit he wore could not have been more ordinary but it also conjured up images of another time and place. In many ways, he could not have looked more like Obi-Wan Kenobi had he tried. The only thing missing was a lightsaber.

As someone who listens to people for a living, I could not help my training from kicking in and attempted to jumpstart the conversation by putting him and myself at ease with polite small talk. Father Eugene would have none of it and jumped right in interrupting me with, "How can I help?" Again, neither friendly nor cold. In many ways this was just another business meeting for him, being in the business of helping people with spiritual matters. No need to waste time on frivolous banter. I had prepared myself for such a question knowing in some way, shape, or form it would come up.

I assumed that people who make the effort to come to this isolated corner of southern Indiana do so for a specific reason. Maybe they have questions about their faith. Maybe they are hurting and lonely and need some guidance. Maybe life just doesn't make sense and they are seeking clarity. I did not fall into any of these categories. I didn't want anything from Father Eugene other than to share a moment in time and possibly gain some wisdom from someone further along the road than myself. I love the quote that we are all just walking each other home. I was perfectly fine sitting with this wise elder monk as we walked each other home for a brief moment in time.

I found out that Father Eugene had been a monk at St. Meinrads since 1961. It was humbling to think of someone so dedicated to a singular path. It also explained a little more about his style of hospitality. He had probably heard it all and that had to take a toll on his soul. I may not have known what I was getting myself into by meeting with a monk but neither did he. He had no idea what burdens I would bring to his doorstep and must prepare himself for anything.

Father Eugene shared that from his experience the reason most people seek out spiritual advice is the sense that something is missing. I explained that I have a full rich life, not without its struggles, but I am content and have a great sense of peace. It was at this moment Father Eugene dropped the first of several wisdom bombs on me.

He said, *"You know the type of person most people want to be around?"*

I shook my head somewhat confused.

"People who are happy and full of joy. Your spiritual life should bring you joy and happiness."

Here we were only a few minutes into our conversation and I felt he had zeroed in on something missing in my life that I was not even aware. I looked away. I looked down. I paused. Father Eugene sat in silence, waiting.

Finally, I managed a slow, methodical response, *"I have spent many years doing my best to live in such a way that brings me peace and I have succeeded. I have a deep, abiding peace in my heart . . . but I wouldn't say I am a joyful person."*

Both of us let my admission hang quietly in the air.

When the moment felt right I asked if I could share my **BE STILL** prayer. Father Eugene agreed and I played a recording of the prayer I set to a melancholy piano melody. I wanted his theological opinions.

After the piano played its final note Father Eugene chimed in, *"I have no problems with it theologically"* he paused, *"But you are so hard on yourself. You've set the bar really high and left no room for human frailty."*

Wisdom Bomb #2.

The humor was not lost on me that I needed a monk to tell me to chill out and lighten up!

Besides the humor, his comments landed somewhere deep. How many times have I heard someone say, *"Reb, you are being too hard on yourself."*

Our conversation caused me to rewrite one sentence in the prayer. Here is the earlier version I shared with Father Eugene:

So often my requests, no matter how sincere, seem to make little difference to the outcome of a situation and only weaken my faith in your goodness and sow seeds of disappointment in my heart. I will never again ask you for anything but forgiveness. Instead, I will meet your silence with my own reverential silence. In this sacred silence, I will seek to be with you, not seek something from you.

Father Eugene recognized that in my zeal to be honest with God, I created a dynamic by which I never speak freely with God about my struggles. This would require the fortitude of a saint and even that would not be enough (and I am no saint).

Sometimes we just need to talk to God to make sense of a situation or just to feel His presence. My intentions were good but he was right in recognizing this would ultimately end in me feeling like a failure for being unable to remain silent with God for the rest of my life.

Father Eugene and I talked about many other topics that day. I even managed to make him laugh at one point. It wasn't one of those polite laughs. He laughed deep from his belly. I counted that as a win.

Father Eugene had one more gift before I left that he didn't even know he was giving me. I am certain he is aware that so much of God's work in interactions such as ours goes unseen by him.

Since being called to a more formal religious life I felt compelled to get rid of many superstitious and magical ideas about God. One example of this fantastical thinking is believing that if I pray in a certain way with earnest sincerity over and over God will be convinced by my persistence. Now I believe that God will act when it is right and God will not act when it is not right regardless of how many times I repeat myself.

At the end of our time together Father Eugene commented, *"The spiritual life is very ordinary."* This is what I heard him say based on his comment and our conversation, *"Reb, you are right to tidy up your spiritual beliefs, bringing them in line with proper theology. Magical thinking only leads to bad outcomes and bad outcomes lead to disappointment. Disappointment can lead to anger and if left to run wild, anger can metastasize into bitterness."*

I am indebted to Father Eugene for his time, his calm presence, and his wisdom. In his own way, he expressed happiness and joy. He gave me the gift of his presence. He saw me in honest, clear ways that I needed and wanted to be seen.

I thought this would be the end of my experience at the monastery as my bags were packed and I was headed home as soon as I left this meeting but there was one more divinely orchestrated experience waiting for me.

Throughout my retreat I passed by the front desk many times. Each time there were the same two friendly faces ready to greet me and offer assistance. Each time I passed we said hello and chatted for a moment. As I was leaving Father Eugene's office I thanked the ladies at the front desk for their hospitality. One of them asked, *"Have you been to the Shrine of Monte Cassino?"* I said I had not and she insisted I go. It was only a mile away and I was under no time constraints so I agreed. I said my goodbyes and drove through the tiniest little dew drop of a town that is Saint Meinrad proper.

The road to the shrine led up a hill through a forest of the most golden autumnal leaves I had ever seen. The forest was full of ochre light and serene beauty. When I arrived at the top I was greeted by a small but stately stone church. I parked and milled around the grounds before entering.

To say I was surprised when I walked inside would be an understatement. Inside this tiny, humble church were arched ceilings covered in frescoes that were as majestic as anything I had seen in Italy. The blues and golds and whites were electric. The marble statues seemed lifelike. The wooden pews and genuflexorium were worn from decades of use. I felt as if I had slipped into a heavenly dream.

At the back of the church were candles and rosaries. I left a few dollars and picked up a pair of royal blue prayer beads (rosaries), lit a candle, and sat down to pray.

It was silent and peaceful and beautiful for a long time. I was sitting in the front of four rows of pews when I heard a small group come in behind me. They lingered for a moment then left. A few minutes later I heard uproarious laughter outside. It didn't bother me but it was loud. After a few moments I decided to leave the quiet comfort of the small cathedral in the woods.

When I opened the creaky wooden door I stepped into a sun-soaked courtyard. There I was greeted by three monks dressed in unusual looking habits all laughing and playing together.

One monk named Brother Gabriel quickly approached me and apologized for disturbing my prayers. I assured him they were not interrupting. He continued to tell me that after seeing me in the chapel they decided to leave but once outside his friend started laughing and could not stop. That is what was causing all the commotion. He even pulled out his phone to show me a funny picture he took of his brother standing at the stone pulpit which was engraved with the words: *Do what he tells you to do.*

The monks and I continued talking. They were Franciscan Friars visiting from Bloomington where they lived at the Mother of the Redeemer Retreat Center. As our conversation unfolded we found there were many similarities. I mentioned being raised in the Assemblies of God and Brother Gabriel said he had just given a retreat for the leadership of an Assembly of God church. I mentioned I had written a prayer and Brother Gabriel shared that in January he was going to be leading a retreat on prayer. This ping-ponging back and forth continued for a while.

Then it dawned on me what Father Eugene attempted to explain when he talked about joy and happiness. These were the happiest monks I had ever met, full of zest, and buzzing with energy. This was the joy Father Eugene was talking about. This moment was divinely orchestrated to bring the abstract idea of joy to life for me.

In a poignant moment, the stark difference between the monks and myself came to light. Brother Gabriel mentioned he wanted to visit Nashville. In an effort to be funny, I joked that he should stay away from downtown if he didn't want to lose his faith in humanity. Without missing a beat and with no judgment at all toward me Brother Gabriel said gently, "Or it would be a good place to witness."

These were two very different worldviews. Mine was to avoid people because they can be rowdy, lewd, and intoxicated. Brother Gabriel's perspective was to care for their souls. It was a humbling experience to see such stark differences being reflected back to me in the mirror Brother Gabriel was holding.

It was as if the monks at St. Meinrads and the monks from Mother of the Redeemer were conspiring on some secret spiritual network to bring about a divinely orchestrated moment for me to not only receive the message that I need more joy and happiness in my spiritual life but to show me what that looks like through real people in an ordinary, everyday situation.

Yes, the spiritual life is ordinary but, at times, it can also be quite extraordinary.

Father Eugene has been a monk at St. Meinrads since 1961.

Saint Meinrad's Archabbey Benedictine Monastery in Saint Meinrad, Indiana.

The interior of the Shrine of Monte Cassino

Photo of Brother Gabriel from the Mother of the Redeemer Retreat Center website

So what?

Why should this matter to you?

It is yet another reminder that miracles often don't arrive with fanfare or fireworks. They often come disguised as choices so small, so ordinary, they're easily overlooked. A casual invitation from two women at a front desk. A fork-in-the-road decision to visit a shrine or beat traffic. On the surface, none of these screams *divine intervention*. But that's exactly the point.

The miracle wasn't just meeting Father Eugene, though it would be easy to headline the story that way: a wise old monk offering soul-shifting guidance. But he was just a part of the scene. The real miracle was in the *whole* thing—the timing, the people, the joy, the way it all came together like a puzzle you didn't know you were putting together.

So what? Because these kinds of experiences happen to all of us *every day*. We stand at the edge of invitations that seem irrelevant, meaningless. And yet, behind some of them, something sacred is waiting. A laugh. A message. A feeling that you're not alone in the universe. That something—or Someone—is actually orchestrating moments for your joy.

And here's the kicker: none of it works without participation. You have to say yes. Not once, but over and over again. You must have an open heart. The alternative—a closed-off, guarded heart—may feel safe, but it numbs you to the beauty, the joy, and yes, the miracles.

So what's the takeaway? God is always doing something, but we have to be awake, quiet, listening to see and hear what is happening. And staying awake means choosing—again and again—not to rush past the ordinary. It means recognizing that the Spirit of Truth doesn't announce itself loudly. It whispers through laughter, nudges through traffic decisions, and sings through unexpected conversations.

No one in my story was the "main character." Not Father Eugene, not the monks, not me. The lead role belonged to the Divine. We were all just extras in a sacred performance. The miracle wasn't a lightning strike—it was the choreography of small, beautiful yeses that created a beautiful moment.

6

THE MIRACLE ON THE GREENWAY

"We all have watershed moments in life, critical turning points where, from that moment on, nothing will ever be the same." This is the opening sentence to Dr. Michael S. Heiser's brilliant book *The Unseen Realm*.

My life can be divided into the time before the miracle on the greenway and the time after. If I had to pick one experience as the most pivotal of my life this would be it.

My rationale for such dramatic language is because what I was given that day allowed me to wake up and truly appreciate and enjoy all the moments of my life. It also made me a better human being.

However, before the light, there was darkness.

There is a reason why Jesus got so flipping angry at the Pharisees and the teachers of the law. They were hypocrites. They said one thing but did another. They burdened others with impossibly high standards under the Pharisaical law while ignoring it themselves. Jesus seemed to loathe this particular flaw of humanity:

> *Woe to you, scribes and Pharisees, hypocrites! For you are like whitewashed tombs, which outwardly appear beautiful, but within are full of dead people's bones and all uncleanness. So you also outwardly appear righteous to others, but within you are full of hypocrisy and lawlessness. -Matthew 23:27 English Standard Version*

The Polaroid version of my life pre-divorce was picture-perfect. The mantle of my marriage and family was, literally and figuratively, full of achievements and milestones. We lived in a beautiful house in a beautiful neighborhood and had beautiful kids. We took beautiful vacations to beautiful beaches and took beautiful family photos in front of beautiful ocean sunsets.

Along with our beautiful life, we had beautiful friendships. We intentionally cultivated deep and meaningful relationships in our community that lasted decades. There were many beautiful, and sometimes courageous, conversations among these friends. We took beautiful trips to beautiful places with these cherished people and created beautiful memories. It was a beautiful time. While the outside looked beautiful, my own inner life was a mess.

If you had asked me if I were a Christian during this time I would have answered, "Yes." Technically, this was true. However, I was more a Pharisee than a follower of Jesus. Behind the scenes of my beautiful life, it was not so beautiful.

As I reflect on that time I have compassion for my younger self. He was lost and didn't even know it. He had no idea he was about to walk head first into a buzz saw that would tear his beautiful life to pieces and it was of his own making.

Internally, I was a frothing toxic caldron of poor choices, unhealthy thinking, and spiritual starvation. I went to church but I only spasmodically opened my heart to God or anyone else. I ignored opportunity after opportunity to save myself and my marriage. Instead of humility, I chose either apathy or arrogance.

Saying I was a whitewashed tomb may sound harsh but it was true. I plead with anyone reading these words to take my life as a warning. Wake up and stop your self-destructive behaviors *before* they take you down. This single act of humility on your part could rescue your life and help you avoid overwhelming pain and suffering. It will also protect those you love the most.

If you are caught in any kind of addiction put this book down right now and find a group for whatever your poison may be. If you are on the verge of having an affair, stop what you are doing immediately and seek help. It will not solve the problems with your marriage, it will exacerbate them. As much as you think you can do this on your own, you can't. If you are living a secretive life choosing gambling, pornography, sex with a sex worker, a coworker, or a stranger over your partner, there are groups such as Sexaholics Anonymous that can walk with you to sobriety.

If your mind is full of selfish, rageful, hateful, judgmental, critical, self-sabotaging, greedy thoughts, turn from that trash and run in the other direction! You may think it's too late for you or too hard but it isn't. Once you make up your mind, you can do anything. What you cannot do is conquer this all by yourself. You are not strong enough and never will be. No one is strong enough and to think you are is foolish.

If you have never experienced divorce, it is utter devastation. Imagine losing money, friends, family, house, a partner, and going to sleep alone at night without your kids and no one to have your back. This is the reality of divorce.

Living with love, wisdom, and integrity is not only about avoiding severe, crippling pain. If you choose love you get to have an amazing, wonderful relationship with your partner filled with hope and joy and more love than you can imagine. You get an authentic, beautiful relationship with your kids, family, friends, and coworkers. You gain true inner peace. This is the miracle waiting for you. All you have to do is turn away from being a whitewashed tomb.

Back to the greenway.

During the divorce, the depression moved in and set up camp. Every day was torture yet I still had clients to see and kids to take care of so I embraced the suck and kept moving forward.

Most of the time I was able to hide my suffering behind a forced smile and small talk but I couldn't hide my body. I remember how the mask I was desperately trying to hide behind kept slipping. A soulful and sensitive client came into my office one day, looked at me, and commented, "Man, you've lost some weight. I hope it's not from divorce." He meant it as a joke but my pain was so close to the surface I couldn't hold back the tears. A few streams managed to sneak past my guard and I shared briefly that I was going through a difficult time in my marriage. He never came back.

One of the best ways I coped with my relentless suffering was walking. I walked and walked and walked and walked. If I wasn't sleeping, working, or with my kids I was walking. I walked in the morning. I walked at night. I walked during breakfast, lunch, and dinner.

It was on one of these ordinary walks that I was given a miracle. I remember everything about that seminal moment. I remember praying and asking for a miracle to save my marriage. I remember praying and asking for God to take away the pain.

As I walked and cried transitioning from a dead-end street in our neighborhood onto the greenway a thought gently entered my mind. I use the word gently because the idea was so subtle I could have easily missed it.

The quiet little whisper said to me, "Love. Wisdom. Integrity." That was it. Nothing else.

I was somewhat confused because I had not been thinking about those words before they came to mind. "Nice," I thought to myself, "those are real nice words." Then I resumed my walking, begging, and pleading with God. Later on the same walk, the whisper returned. This time it came with a tiny little instruction manual.

The whisper said to me a second time, "From this day forward for the rest of your life live each day with love, wisdom, and integrity."

"Oh! Those words were for me!" It was as if my entire body lit up like a night sky on the 4th of July. Mere minutes before I had been in a pit of despair but this idea of love, wisdom, and integrity sent a megawatt of positivity coursing through my mind and body. The reason for such a strong reaction was because I knew instinctively this one sentence was not simply a nice idea, it was an answer to prayer that would save my life. It was the solution I needed. This would be my ticket out of the hell on earth I had created. It was my path to freedom and redemption. It was how I would find healing.

I imagine what I felt at the moment was similar to what a prisoner must feel walking out of prison a free man. The liberation was intoxicating.

I give credit to God for arranging this experience. I did not conjure it up on my own. This didn't come from a podcast, book, or even my therapist. This came from somewhere beyond my own mind and beyond this world.

I cannot tell you all the big and small ways this shift has changed my life for the better. Along with adopting these virtues as my mantra, I integrated them into my work. I talk about them constantly with clients. What I came to realize is that many people have one of these virtues. A lot of people even have two of them. But many people struggle to have all three. It takes all three to be whole.

For example, if you are wise and have integrity but you are not loving, you will be harsh and judgmental. If you have love and wisdom but do not combine it with integrity, you will be reckless. If you have integrity and love . . . well, you'll probably be okay.

I have not lived every moment since this experience perfectly with love, wisdom, and integrity. The beauty of this virtuous trio is that they are not only helpful to know how to live every day but they are also the path to understanding where and how you messed up and what needs to be fixed. In other words, when you mess up, you know which path will make things right.

I encourage you to adopt these virtues as your way of living. Make them an integral part of your everyday life. Very quickly you will start to see how helpful they are with making decisions, your relationships, your work, your spiritual life, your children, etc.

When I mess up, my children will sometimes use my mantra of love, wisdom, and integrity to poke fun at me. And you know what? I love it. It's good for a laugh. While they think they are pranking me, I know little by little as they say those words out loud they are taking them into their heart, mind, and body. I couldn't ask for anything better than to know my pain and the lessons I have learned will in some way help my kids avoid at least some unnecessary pain and suffering.

Each morning I put a chain around my neck that has three objects. There is a St. Meinrads medallion. There is a small round piece I found on the ground that has a tree of life on one side and the quote, "Family is where love grows" on the other. There is a circle with a triangle inside. This has become my symbol for love, wisdom, and integrity.

I created a mantra to remind me every day of how I want to live. Feel free to borrow it for yourself. The mantra is:

May I be loving

May I seek wisdom

May I act with integrity

May I have a courageous heart

Morning on the greenway where I received the message to live with love, wisdom, and integrity

Necklace I put on every morning to remind me of my values

So What?

Why should this matter to you?

If something life-changing can happen to me, it can happen to you. That's not just a feel-good idea—it's a truth that has the power to sustain you when nothing else can.

Here's the reality: pain is guaranteed. What's not guaranteed is *what you do with it*. You can let it harden you, break you, define you—or you can let it wake you up. You can let it be the soil where healing and transformation grow. And that choice? That's yours to make.

So what does it take to transform pain into healing? For me, it boiled down to this simple truth: If you want to avoid unnecessary suffering, live by love, wisdom, and integrity. It sounds simple. But it's everything. When I've lived by those virtues, my life has flourished. When I haven't, it has unraveled. That's not a theory. That's experience.

So what can you do right now, especially if you're stuck in suffering or feel like you're on the edge of losing your beautiful life?

1. **Humble Yourself.** Stop pretending you're supposed to carry it all alone. Ask for help. It's not weakness—it's strength in disguise.

2. **Open Your Heart.** Even if it's just a sliver, that opening creates space for light to get in. That's how change starts.

3. **Return To Daily Spiritual Practices.** Not because they check boxes, but because they anchor you. Prayer, reflection, journaling —these reconnect you to the source of healing and wisdom.

4. **Run From Evil.** Not negotiate with it. Not flirt with it. Run. Because what you allow into your life shapes what your life becomes.

So what? Because your suffering doesn't have to end in despair. It can be the doorway to a life of strength, clarity, and deep joy. But only if you choose to walk through that door.

Keep holding on to hope. Keep living with love, wisdom, and integrity as your compass. You don't need to have it all figured out. You just need to stay open to what's possible—and take the next right step.

7

THE MIRACLE OF THE NOTE FROM GOD

Throughout high school I couldn't shake the feeling that I did not belong in the small, rural southern town where I lived. I just didn't fit in. Most guys at my high school were tough guys. They drove pickup trucks and wore camouflage all year round. During hunting season many of them often arrived with dead deer on their hoods and a .30-06 Winchester rifle racked in the back window.

I, on the other hand, drove a red convertible 1966 Mustang. I had a vanity license plate with WALL ST on it based on the movie by the same name. I carried a briefcase to school instead of a backpack and read the Wall Street Journal between classes. As further evidence of my shallow, materialistic tendencies, one Easter I bought myself a Gucci watch as an Easter gift to myself because you know, that's what Easter is all about! I have a truck load full of compassion when I think about that young man.

In high school I played baseball and tennis. I was offered a scholarship to play tennis on the practice squad for the University of Southern Mississippi (Southern). The sister of my mixed doubles partner worked at the university and offered us the opportunity after watching us play. I don't remember wrestling much with the decision but I declined the offer in favor of going to the University of Alabama (Alabama). Some say you shouldn't regret any decision because it made you the person you are today. I don't agree with that statement. Rejecting the scholarship and going to Alabama ranks as the second worst decision I have ever made and I do regret it.

The sole reason for choosing Alabama over Southern was singular and shallow. I wanted to impress my friends. Seeing the look of approval, and maybe a little jealousy, on their faces when I told them my choice of colleges was the only criteria that mattered to me. What I was unaware of at the time but would learn in a very painful and humiliating way was that Alabama only had three types of students: the jocks, the geeks, and the greeks. I would fall into none of those categories and once again find myself an outsider.

Once at Alabama, I learned about open tryouts for the tennis team where anyone could compete for a spot on the team. My hopes ran high until I was embarrassingly defeated on the first day. It was devastating. On the walk back to my dorm, a sinking feeling emerged that maybe I had made a bad decision. The year turned out to be a disaster.

My sudden elimination from the tennis team was the first of many blows to my ego. This eliminated me from the jock category. Strike one.

In high school I never learned the art and science of studying. Everyone can be good at academics if they try. Some people just have to try harder than others to get the same results. I never gave myself the chance to thrive. This eliminated me from the geek category. Strike two.

I could have bought my way into the Greek fraternity system but my conservative Christian parents refused to subsidize a life of excess and debauchery. It was up to me to pay the $5,000 per semester fee if I wanted to join. That was impossible, eliminating me from the greek category. Strike three.

Making friends was hard because I didn't have an identity. This made weekends painfully lonely. I quickly became depressed but it never occurred to me to reach out for help or talk to a counselor. By Christmas Break, I developed stomach ulcers, living in a hell of my own creation

I returned home for the summer with my tail tucked between my legs and no tennis scholarship. However, I had to make it through the summer which turned out to be more difficult and humiliating than I anticipated.

When I moved back in with my parents I needed a job. A friend's father owned a restaurant in the local mall selling corn dogs. I needed the money and accepted the opportunity. I can remember one of the most humiliating experiences of my life up to that point was when I was asked to take out the restaurant's garbage.

The restaurant had no back door leading to the alley. To accomplish this task I had to roll each smelly, industrial sized garbage container one by one down the main corridor where everyone walked. My friends, whom I wanted so desperately to impress, were home on their summer breaks. The mall was the place to hang out, go to a movie, or grab a quick bite to eat. All summer long I greeted a steady stream of friends, each one looking happy and healthy, while I was pale and much too thin wearing an apron with a smiling corn dog on it. I was beyond embarrassed. More Mike Tyson gut punches to the ego. My self-esteem could not have been lower.

Summer dragged on until finally Fall came to my rescue. I enrolled in classes at Southern and quickly made friends. For the first time in a long time it felt as if I had finally made a good decision. It didn't take long before I got involved in extracurricular activities. I had my own radio show on the local college station. I was doing well in classes. I was meeting lots of cool, new people and went on a few dates. I sought out and became involved in a faith-based group called Campus Crusade for Christ (CCC). Life was thankfully returning to normal.

As the semester came to a close for the Christmas holiday the staff for CCC started to put pressure on us to consider spending the coming summer break on a mission trip called a Summer Project. To rev up excitement about the Summer Projects they convinced a group of students who regularly attended the weekly meetings to go to a national conference over the Christmas break. This particular year it was to be held in Dallas, Texas. Each year thousands of college students from all over the nation attended this gathering. My parents were more than willing to foot the bill for me to spend a little time with Jesus in Texas.

These conventions were high-energy events with well known speakers and popular Christian musicians. There were meetings held throughout the week intended to recruit students to spend their summer months on a mission trip somewhere around the globe. Other meetings focused on recruiting potential new staff members to the organization after graduation.

Ken was the CCC staff member assigned to be my mentor. During one of the sessions we watched a video about a Summer Project in Yellowstone National Park. When it was over Ken encouraged me to get involved, "Just fill out the paperwork," he said, "You can cancel later if you decide not to go." I applied and was accepted. I was going to Yellowstone!

School ended in May and in a matter of days I was on a plane to Wyoming. Our group of forty students spent the first week in beautiful Jackson Hole at a dude ranch getting to know one another and preparing for the three months ahead in Yellowstone. The point of all Summer Projects was to save lost souls. We were technically park employees but our mission was to convert other staff and visitors to Christianity. Needless to say, we were received with a great deal of suspicion by the rest of the park staff.

Our CCC crew was a close knit group. Soon enough I found myself smitten with a lovely young lady named Ethel. She had long curly brown hair and definitely checked all the boxes for a Granola Girl. Ethel was naturally beautiful and wore no makeup. She didn't wear flashy clothes or name brand hiking apparel. She was smart, kind, and funny.

Word made it back to my group of guy friends that Ethel liked someone in our group. Being a good Christian, plus being on a mission trip to boot, I felt I should pray for guidance on whether or not to tell Ethel how I felt about her.

My original job in the park was cleaning cabins between visitors or "tourons" as the staff called them. The crass term was a combination of tourist and moron and came from the epic lengths of recklessness some tourists would go to get their photograph with a bear, bison, or moose.

Housekeeping included everything no one would ever want to do: scrubbing showers, cleaning toilets, mopping floors, vacuuming, making beds, and a host of other small but important tasks.

My supervisor, who loathed us Christians, came to observe me one day. He asked me questions about myself as we went to each cabin. He eventually engaged me in a light discussion of Christianity. "Man," I thought to myself, "I'm really doing missionary work! I'm witnessing to someone who isn't saved." He asked some difficult questions and I thought I was on the road to bagging my first non-believer. At the end of my shift he told me not to come back to the housekeeping division.

I was too slow. I was going to be on the grounds keeping team now. Without even realizing it, I became a terrible example of a Christian reinforcing my supervisor's negative stereotype.

The ground crew job was a lot of fun. I woke up early to keep the grounds neat and tidy. One of my jobs was to pick up trash with a long stick that had a pointy end to poke the trash.

Unofficially, I was a tour guide. The tourists who were early risers would seek me out on their morning strolls. They wanted to know where I was from, the best hiking trails, and the best place to take a picture of the famous falls. I shared what I knew and engaged them in conversation.

During the day when the tourists were out seeing the wonders of the park I had long hours alone. It was during these quieter times that I would pray about Ethel. Should I or should I not tell Ethel how I felt about her? As the days turned into weeks the notion that she and I could be a couple dominated my thoughts. I set out each day asking God what I should do.

In spite of all my immaturity and lack of spiritual depth, I was truly sincere in my prayers. However, looking back now I realize I was only seeking confirmation for what I wanted, not what was best for me or Ethel or even what God wanted.

I prayed every day asking God if I should share my feelings with Ethel. When no answer came I prayed more. Day after day I kept praying and picking up trash until one day God wrote me a note.

On this particular day I had wandered far behind the cabins into the nearby woods. The isolated area was perfect for praying. I could talk openly to God without worrying about anyone hearing me. The weather was nice and I had nothing but time. I tossed up my usual fare of something like, "God, should I tell Ethel how I feel?"

As I uttered the prayer I stabbed a plain white piece of paper with my wooden poker stick. Much to my amazement written on the piece of trash in large blue capital letters was the word, "NO".

I laughed out loud. It was the kind of silly, gut-busting laughter that threatens to overtake the whole body. My very first thought was "This can't be a note from God. Whoever heard of God writing people notes?" After my laughing subsided I tossed the little note in the trash and went on about my day.

That evening I recounted the experience to my roommate. He asked to see the note and then it hit me: I had thrown away a note from God! We laughed at the incredulity of my irresponsibility and the hilarity of God communicating to me through a piece of trash. What was much more egregious was my careless disregard of the note's message.

After a few days I decided that this young lady was much too important than a silly note that was maybe/maybe not from God. In a bold act of defiance I marched over to Ethel's dorm to share my feelings.

I went to her dorm room and knocked on the door. She answered with her naturally beautiful smile and I melted. I asked if I could speak with her and she said enthusiastically, "Sure!" inviting me into her room. We are off to a great start, I thought.

Her roommate was gone which I took as further confirmation I was on the right path. For a while we bantered back and forth about hikes and trails and the latest CCC gossip. Then, with all the confidence I could muster, I told her that I thought she was pretty, that she had a wonderful personality, and that I would like to get to know her better. That was it. It took less than twenty seconds.

As I shared my feelings, the mood in the room dramatically shifted from warm and inviting to cold and awkward. She withdrew and became visibly uncomfortable. She could not hide her discomfort from contorting her face. I sensed her agony and not knowing what to do I panicked. The only thing I could think to do was say more.

The more I talked the more the distance between us grew. I don't remember what she said but the look of shock remained. I remember leaving and feeling embarrassed as if I had done something wrong. Ethel and I were way out of sync about our feelings for each other.

The next morning during breakfast I saw her walk into the cafeteria and get in line. As she exited with her tray our eyes met. She immediately turned the other way as fast as humanly possible while carrying a tray full of food. My heart sank. Her answer was no, not me. God's note was confirmed. I had taken my own path and created a mess.

Weeks passed with the awkwardness hanging in the air. I had directly disobeyed a clear answer to prayer while on a mission trip attempting to evangelize to others to pray and listen to God. I also lost a good friend. We no longer hung out together. We no longer took hikes in the back country. There was a small but significant division in our group because of this unfortunate and avoidable situation.

One evening after one of our big group meetings everyone was sitting around talking. At this point my ego was so damaged that I flat out ignored Ethel any time our paths crossed.

As a testament to Ethel's integrity she moved into the hard place of confronting the awkwardness. As I sat clustered together among my friends I remember feeling a presence behind me. I turned and standing behind me was Ethel. She had soft, forgiving eyes and asked me tenderly, "Can we talk?" I acted like a fool pretending absolutely nothing was wrong. I said a little too enthusiastically, "Sure. What's up? How are you?" She tilted her head sideways giving me the "You've got to be kidding" look. I finally exhaled a deep sigh. With that breath of acknowledgment, my body slumped from the exhaustion of carrying so much shame.

Ethel sat down and we hashed out what happened when I came to her room. I told her the story of my praying and the note I had received from God. She simultaneously felt angry at my stubbornness and entertained at the divine comedy of it all. I asked her forgiveness. She graciously accepted and our relationship was restored . . . almost.

While I believe that we were both sincere in the giving and receiving of forgiveness, the awkwardness between us never completely evaporated. The guy who the rumors were about that I erroneously thought were about me was a truly great man. They became a couple that summer and eventually married.

I have a particular fondness for this story. It not only tells of the funny and playful nature of God, it reveals a message that not even when we ignore God are his efforts wasted. Had I heeded the message it would have saved all involved a lot of heartache. But would I still be talking about this story? Maybe. I mean God did write me a note!

The original note was thrown in the trash. This is a replica of what the note looked like

SO WHAT?

Why should this matter to you?

This is not just a sweet story about unrequited love or a well-timed prayer being answered. It's a story about alignment—of heart, timing, desire, and divine orchestration. And it raises a crucial question: *Are you paying attention when your miracle shows up?*

Yes, prayer works. That's the headline. But the deeper story is about *what happens when you're ready to receive what you've prayed for.* If Ethel hadn't been in a healthy, grounded place—emotionally and spiritually—my actions might have confused her. She could have followed the wrong cues and missed the real connection with her future husband.

Desire is powerful—and holy. It's part of being human to crave connection, to feel awakened by another person. But when we chase that spark without discernment—cut off from God, from community, from wisdom—we risk getting burned.

That's why it matters to stay open-hearted and not isolated. To desire deeply, but also to stay grounded in feedback from God and others. Real love isn't something we just stumble into. It's something we recognize when we're spiritually awake and emotionally healthy enough to notice the signs.

Here's another so what: when you mess up, *own it.* Don't let guilt fester. Don't ghost the problem. Avoidance doesn't protect your peace—it just postpones your chaos. Whatever you ignore today will become the chaos of tomorrow.

And maybe most importantly: if God sends you a message—don't dismiss it. Miracles rarely, if ever, come wrapped in thunderclaps. The majority of the time they come as a quiet moment, a subtle nudge, a person who crosses your path when you least expect it. But if you're too distracted, too afraid, or too self-absorbed, you might miss it altogether.

8

THE MIRACLE OF NOT GOING

I almost graduated from the University of Southern Mississippi in May of 1994. I say almost because after one year at Alabama and three years at Southern I made a D in a very difficult macroeconomics class I needed to graduate. I was so over school by this point I didn't hang around to take it again. I knew I would get to it at some point and I did.

My years at Southern were good. There were the typical tumultuous romantic flings and normal crises young people go through at that age but overall I have fond memories of that time.

I began my college career as a Banking & Finance major. However, during my junior year I started asking myself if a career in business was what I really wanted to do the rest of my life. Did I want a 9-5 office job? My answer was absolutely not but I was conflicted. Only a few short years before I was the young rebel who acted counterculture by being the preppy kid in a redneck school who carried a briefcase rather than a can of Skoal. What changed? My business classes were of zero interest. In fact, they bored me. I had no passion for economic theories and accounting methods.

After my Yellowstone experience I now sported shoulder-length hair and Birkenstock sandals. These were not typical business school attire. What was more unsettling was I didn't know what I wanted to do. This sea of uncertainty set me up for a semester of venturing to see what other opportunities my university had to offer.

I looked into getting a Philosophy degree. I considered switching to Food, Nutrition, and Sports Science. I considered a degree in Psychology but ultimately decided against that too. The course of study I found most intriguing during this walkabout was the Forestry and Land Management department. A degree from this college would allow me to become a park ranger.

It was about this time my father realized my aimless wandering was going to keep me in school for at least another year, maybe two. He was adamant that he was not going to foot the bill for that. Out of necessity, I ended up back where I began taking business classes so I could graduate and get on with life.

At the end of May 1994 my father told me that I could no longer live with my grandparents. I needed to find my own place. I had no idea where to go or what to do. I knew I liked music and I knew from visiting Nashville once that it seemed a decent enough city. So I packed my bags and headed north.

I worked at the world famous Bluebird Cafe and met celebrities while hanging out in the kitchen. The staff were a hodgepodge of Vietnam War vets, Bio-Chem Majors, black belts in karate, and rising Honky Tonk stars. There were some memorable nights of fun but I knew I needed to move on.

I decided to get a better paying job because it was better than living in my car during the winter. Through a friend I was hired by a financial management firm that specialized in professional musicians and athletes. I stayed in that job for three and a half years. The work was boring but my coworkers were fun. I had regular interactions with famous people from the entertainment and sports world that made the long stretches of monotony tolerable.

About two and a half years into my tenure with this firm I became restless. During the Spring I could think of nothing I wanted more than to be outside. However, I was shackled to my desk reconciling bank statements, and matching credit card receipts to a tour manager's sloppily scribbled notes on manila envelopes. It was time to move on again but I was plagued by the question: What do I do? It was time for me to go on another walkabout.

I began asking everyone what they did, did they like it, and how they decided on their profession. Each story was unique to the individual with layers of nuance and providence woven into each twist and turn.

After a year's long search I felt pulled to graduate school with an emphasis on counseling. I had to make a few major big boy decisions at this point such as when to go and what graduate school to attend. It didn't take me long to land on Colorado Christian University. I was thrilled because this accomplished two life goals. First, I had direction about what I was going to do with my life. Second, I always wanted to live in Colorado.

A few weeks before I left for Colorado my friends threw a going away party and with that party my life in Nashville came to a happy, yet melancholy, end. After the party, I had a few weeks before I could move into my dorm room so I stayed with my parents. Within a few days of moving home the heaviest, darkest depression settled on me.

Besides being depressed I had a sense of dread growing stronger each day. What was I dreading? Hadn't I just spent the past year discerning what I was supposed to do with my life? Didn't I just make huge sacrifices by quitting my job and leaving the house I was renting with friends? Didn't everything line up in this process signalling I was making the right decision? Why was it all falling apart?

It didn't feel like moving to Colorado was the right thing to do. However, the idea of not going was highly disorienting, deeply confusing, and very scary. How could I cancel my plans now? What would I do? I was frozen in terror. I imagined the humiliation of moving back to Nashville and having to explain again and again, "Just kidding. I didn't go to grad school. Now, who needs a roommate!?"

With only a few weeks before my planned departure I decided to spend a few days with my good friend Jim. I drove back to Nashville and slept on his couch. We discussed my dilemma over peanut butter and jelly sandwiches. He listened as I waffled, prayed, and complained about my predicament.

During that week I read the book, *Do It! Let's Get Off Our Buts*, by John-Roger and Peter McWilliams. The subtitle is *A Guide To Living Your Dreams*. I did not know this when I began reading it but the purpose of the book was to help motivate those struggling with depression. It was an entertaining read and timely for me as I needed something positive to counter my growing despair.

Then I received a clue in the form of subtle yet clear thought.

One day I found myself in Jim's kitchen making another peanut butter and jelly sandwich once again going over my options. At some point a flood of thoughts began to cascade one after the other into my consciousness. I began to see how I was manufacturing my own dilemma. I had built up the expectations of others so high that I couldn't imagine letting them down or more accurately letting others think less of me. What would others think if I didn't go to Colorado? Could I get my old job back? What would I tell my friends? The questions rolled like waves on the beach, one after the other.

At one point my thoughts crystalized into a series of obvious facts. I was the one that was going to have to sit in the classes. I was the one that was taking out the loans. I was the one that would have to pay back those loans. Just pondering these obvious facts felt like escaping a smoke filled room. Not only could I breathe again but I felt like I had narrowly escaped a burning building. For the first time I now felt I had the power and freedom to choose my own destiny because I was the one responsible for making the choices and living with my decisions.

In a moment of clarity I realized my fear of what my friends and family would think of me if I didn't go was a new twist on an old unhealthy dynamic harkening back to my decision about which college to attend. The egotistical mindset that foiled me into going to Alabama was again at play but in this round I was fighting back and winning.

Just realizing I had options was a good and necessary step but it wasn't actually a decision. I still had to decide if I was moving to Colorado or not. Time was ticking closer and closer to the first day of classes.

As the final week before classes were to start came to an end, I knew I had to make a decision. With my newfound freedom I prayed for wisdom, read my book, and talked to Jim. Time kept marching forward. While my sense of dread lightened somewhat it still hung around me like the scent of a smoker who has left the room.

It was during this painful period of waiting that I finally heard a clear message from the God that I so desperately needed. The message was simple, "You can go, but don't go." I remember feeling underwhelmed. That's obvious, isn't it? I knew I could go and I knew I could not go. What difference did it make if those two ideas were smashed together?

I sat on the couch and pondered this message for a very long time. Was the "You can go" permission to go and the "Don't go" meant there was something more waiting for me if I didn't go? I wondered why the need for a conditional statement at all. Why not just say, "Don't go."

I came to the conclusion that this *was* a message from God. It had the tell-tale signs of peace and the freedom to choose. I knew what I needed to do but it was still a struggle to make the choice. The looming question in my mind was if I don't go to Colorado what do I do? I couldn't return to my job. I didn't have a place to live.

As bad as those dreadful realities were, I knew what I needed to do. I had to stay. When I turned off the idea of going to Colorado the weight of the entire world lifted from my shoulders immediately. I could literally take in a full breath for the first time in a very long time. My countenance lightened. My spirits were flying high. It was the right decision and I felt it in my bones. I felt how Scrooge must have felt on Christmas day in Charles Dickens' *A Christmas Carol*, "I am as light as a feather, I am as happy as an angel, I am as merry as a schoolboy. I am as giddy as a drunken man."

I made the hard decision to move back to Nashville and face the endless questions of, "How's school going?" with the answer, "I didn't go . . ." A few weeks after I returned to Nashville I asked my ex wife on a date. While our marriage didn't make it, there were so many great things about it. We taught each other a lot and grew up together. She gave me the second greatest gift in my life which were our four incredible children.

If I had to do it all over again knowing in the end I would get four amazing children and one divorce I would make the same choices. I would not go to Colorado. I would marry my ex wife. I would go through a divorce. That is how much I love my children and value what our marriage and divorce gave me.

The actual book I read twenty seven years ago during my time of discernment on my friend's couch

So What?

Why should this matter to you?

Sometimes, the clearest messages from God don't come through words or signs—it comes through the body. That is how wisdom got my attention. On the surface, everything looked like it was lining up perfectly. A move to Colorado. A fresh start. Every external sign said "Go!" But my body said *NO!* And thankfully, I listened.

So what? Because it's easy to mistake momentum for clarity and truth. It's easy to convince yourself that doubt is weakness, and all you need is more grit. But sometimes, doubt *is* the message. Sometimes, pain *is* divine redirection.

I didn't know what God knew. I had a purpose yet to be discovered. If I had overridden my inner knowing, if I had pushed past my depression and moved forward anyway I would've walked straight past so many blessings and miracles.

So what? Because you might be in a similar place right now. You might feel stuck, uncertain, or like the thing you were so sure about suddenly doesn't sit right. Don't dismiss that discomfort. And don't go through it alone.

Discerning your path—your calling, your vocation—is rarely straightforward. Some people know early on, but many don't. Life throws curve balls. Dreams crash. Plans unravel. But *that* doesn't mean you're lost. It just means you need to listen more deeply.

When everything felt unclear to me, I did the only wise thing I could: I got still. I found a quiet space—literally a friend's couch—and gave my heart, mind, body, and soul the chance to speak. And they did.

So what? Because maybe the best thing you can do right now isn't hustle harder or panic over finding your "calling." Maybe it's to pause. Get still. Let your body speak. Invite wisdom in—especially from people who aren't tangled up in your emotions or your fears. That kind of perspective is priceless.

9

THE MIRACLE OF THE BULLET & SIPPY CUP

Not every miracle in this book is tied up neatly with a bow and a happy ending. This is a tragic story full of darkness and evil. One of the many miracles in this story is the fact that I survived an attempted murder on my life while my children were hiding in a closet upstairs.

The first time I saw the Germantown neighborhood near downtown Nashville I knew I wanted to live there. It possessed a timeless, enchanting charm with deep history. Each street in the diminutive neighborhood had impeccably restored Victorian era homes side-by-side with shotgun row houses.

Historically, the neighborhood was occupied by wealthy German aristocrats who lived next door to their servants and other working class folk. It is a unique area of Nashville rich with history.

Today it has been revitalized and, much like its history, the ornate mansions of the past have been restored to their grandeur and are now located next to government subsidized housing. The rich and poor are, once again, reunited.

There is a large factory called the Werthan Building on the northern edge of the eighteen block neighborhood. Just beyond the Werthan Building lies Salemtown, a newer community with less ostentatious homes but a complex history all its own. It is Germantown's red-headed step sister.

As I drove around Germantown stopping to pick up those little information sheets in the tubes of the For Sale signs, I quickly realized the prices were three times higher than those in Salemtown. The factory protected Germantown against the rampant criminal activity so prevalent mere blocks away and that was worth a lot of money.

My ex wife and I were living in a small, poorly laid out home near one of the universities in Nashville. It was a quiet neighborhood for the most part as our street sat off the main thoroughfare.

There were a few problems with the home. The kitchen was long and narrow and not well suited for entertaining. There was no dining room. A creek ran alongside the house that was charming to look at but was often filled with snakes. More than once I walked to the water's edge only to have a snake fall from a low limb into the water. Our neighbors were young adults who smoked various substances and had tumultuous personal lives. All these frustrations led us to wanting a place of our own.

As we began to play around with the idea of buying a home, Germantown was my first choice. As I drove her through the neighborhood she too fell under its charming spell. The only problem was we could not afford any of the homes. Owning our limitations, we turned our attention to the less desirable but more affordable Salemtown. Immediately we found a new construction home in our price range.

My ex wife and I were willing to roll up our sleeves and do as much work as possible to save a little money. One way we thought we could save a few bucks was to forgo hiring a real estate agent.

We put an offer on the house and once the negotiations began, we leveraged the seller's agent to become our agent by proxy. She wanted the sale. We didn't want to pay the agent's fee. It worked for everyone! The builder wanted to sell the property and didn't care one way or the other.

The glaring obvious failure of our half-witted plan was that no one was looking out for our best interests. We weren't real estate professionals. We were cheap to the point of being dangerous and that nearly cost me my life.

We were doe-eyed dreamers when we did the walk-through one beautiful Sunday morning. It was sunny and the morning dew was still fresh on the grass. The neighborhood had a quiet, sleepy feel. When we stepped in the front door we were met with the smell of fresh paint and varnish on the new hardwood floors. We were enchanted.

We talked about where the dining room table would go and how we needed a new sofa. In our minds the house was ours and we had already moved in. Reflecting later, we realized that one of our many mistakes was not walking or driving the neighborhood at night.

We left the showing with fantasies of purchasing the home as an investment property. We would live in it for X amount of time then either flip it for $X profit or keep it and become landlords.

The neighborhood was booming with activity. New houses were being built and sold for or above their asking price. Old houses were being razed and shiny new condominiums going up on every corner. We felt we were on the bleeding edge of the vibrant housing economy in Nashville and were perched to make a large profit in a short amount of time. Before long, however, the warning signs started screaming at us.

One of the first warning signs to appear was in our mortgage lenders office while signing all the paperwork. I am a stickler for reading every word before signing a contract. Anyone who has ever bought a house knows there is an encyclopedias worth of paperwork to go through. As I thumbed through each page I knew I didn't understand half the legalese but I asked appropriate questions and signed or initialed as needed.

On the very last page I notice a box wasn't checked that should have been. I brought this to the mortgage brokers attention. The flat look on her face showed something like disappointment mingled with annoyance. She mumbled a few words underneath her breath then checked the box. We were then informed that because of that little box being checked someone would now have to do a second visual inspection of the property.

There was a small part of me that felt proud I was "paying attention to the details". With my chest puffed up we left her office with the impression that this was just a minor issue that would resolve itself quickly.

This "minor issue" turned into an earthquake of a problem. That one little box resulted in the mortgage company having to do another inspection which unearthed one problem after another. It was as if I pulled on a string and before I knew it the whole sweater lay unraveled at my feet.

The broker called to inform us that the builder who was also the seller was not certified by the FHA. He didn't get the plans approved prior to building the house which meant it couldn't be approved for FHA lending. There was one loophole. He would need to purchase a special type of insurance specifically for builders.

As we did not have an agent and did not have the wisdom to seek one out at this major juncture, I was left to clean up the mess.

Dutifully, I began negotiations with the builder/seller via his agent. Conversations passed back and forth until the builder decided he didn't want to fill out all the paperwork. I agreed to fill it out for him. Then he didn't want to pay the several hundred dollars. I agreed to write that into the final contract. I was then told that the builder decided against getting the insurance. This caused me a great amount of frustration. Why the sudden change of heart? It made no sense. His agent eventually confided that this special insurance for builders required a background check and he could not pass it. The pile of warning flags on the front lawn were getting bigger and bigger. Where some people would have seen warning signs, I only saw an obstacle I needed to overcome. It never crossed my mind that maybe I should pause and ask if buying this house was the right decision.

More problems emerged faster than I could solve. Every day I was playing the whack-a-problem game. The mortgage broker gave us the disappointing news that due to the builder/sellers refusal to cooperate we would need a new kind of financing. We would have to redo all the paperwork for a third time. My ex wife and I talked and agreed this was just the complicated and confusing process of buying a home. We instructed the broker to move forward with the new financing.

The night before the morning we were to close we received a call from our mortgage broker, "I've got bad news," she began, "the financing didn't go through." I thought my head would explode with rage. I became insufferable and rudely reprimanded her in a verbally abusive rant. I complained that everyone in this deal had a place to go home to tomorrow night but my family. This was technically true but we had many other practical options.

It would have been wise to take a step way back and look at the big picture but we didn't. I allowed my immaturity and emotions to go unchecked. After finishing the call, I phoned the seller's agent and gave her a piece of my mind about her client's seedy tactics. She agreed and let me rant. I called the mortgage broker back and told her to make it work no matter what. We were moving into that house tomorrow. She was getting tired of my immature, disrespectful rants and shot back, "Fine! Be in my office at four!"

It was touch and go the next day as the broker worked feverishly to get our new financing approved. Around three in the afternoon we received the call that it had finally been approved. The closing was scheduled in an hour. We arrived at the lawyer's office energized. I congratulated myself with the belief that I had persevered through it all. I was victorious. My family would have a home!

We signed the necessary paperwork and were handed the keys to our new home. To our surprise and to my chagrin the builder/seller walked around the corner with his agent extending his hand. I remember the wide grin and casual ease with which he carried himself. We later found out he was also a preacher. I shook his hand but quickly turned away.

That evening our little family of four went to our new house and ordered pizza. We sat on the floor of our new home and gave thanks to God for providing for us. We asked for God to protect us in our new home. We would need that prayer far more than we could have ever imagined.

The house was two stories with 10' foot high ceilings and large windows that overlooked downtown Nashville. The windows were so large we were afraid our toddlers might fall through them or out of them. We started finding small details indicative of slipshod workmanship. Bigger problems would emerge with plumbing and other structural elements but those turned out to be the least of our worries.

The second night we stayed at the house I was awakened by a loud knocking on the front door. Reluctantly, I made my way downstairs and saw a large scantily clad African American woman standing outside. She was disheveled and intoxicated. I opened the door and she bellowed in her drunken stupor, "Can I borrow a dollar for some gas?" I was so groggy I just stood there until my ex wife yelled from the bedroom, "Shut the door!" I did and the lady chuckled as she staggered away.

A few days later I was awakened by the low rumbling bass of a car audio system. I peaked out the window to see a group of young men standing around a car drinking. They were our neighbors. The bass continued for another hour and I became angry but I was also afraid. If I confronted them it might not turn out well. I did nothing except lie there fuming.

A few weeks after that incident I found myself sitting on the couch reading a book. It was around eleven at night and everyone else was in bed. As I read I heard popping and snapping. It was late August and I wondered who was still shooting fireworks so long after the 4th of July. I rolled off the couch and casually sauntered down the hallway. The back door to the house was double glass-panelled doors with thick white vinyl blinds. The blinds were drawn giving me an unobstructed view of our backyard and the busy main thoroughfare across the church parking lot behind our house.

Each time I roll through these memories they play out in slow motion. I walked down the hall and heard the same cracking sound but louder.

I saw the repeated flash of what I knew to be the flower-like pattern emitted from the muzzle of a gun. In horror I realized I was seeing someone shoot a gun not hearing fireworks. What I saw and heard came into unison when I realized that someone was unloading a clip full of ammunition in the alley behind our house.

As I saw the flashes of fire coming from the barrel I panicked believing the shooter was pointing the gun in my direction. My mind adjusted and quickly realized the shooter's back was to me and he was firing into the government subsidized housing across a very busy thoroughfare. My fear of being shot turned to panic knowing there was a man with a gun shooting outside my house. I ran upstairs and grabbed my daughter and tossed her in bed with my ex wife. I ran back to get our other daughter but before I grabbed her I peeked through the blinds and saw three men with guns climbing over the neighbor's fence.

Being raised around guns I knew exactly what I was seeing. One of the guns was a 12 gauge pump shotgun, another was either a real or replica of an AK-47 with its characteristic curved ammo clip and wooden stock and hand grip, the other was a 9mm pistol. They were passing these guns to one another so the other person could climb the fence. A wave of fear and despair overwhelmed me. Not only was there one guy with a pistol, there were three and they all had very dangerous weapons. I carried my other daughter to our bed and lay down in fear after having experienced the worst night of my life. In a few short weeks I would be involved in an even more terrifying experience.

The next morning my ex wife and I sat on the couch in shock. What was there to say? The night before was not a bad nightmare we could forget. It really happened. We just purchased the house and didn't see any way out. We knew we couldn't stay but how do we exit? We were paralyzed with fear with no good options.

The shootings continued. Most of them were blocks away but I learned to estimate how close the shooter might be, what type of guns were used, and in what direction they were shooting just in case we needed to find cover or run away.

Every few weeks there would be a news report of a body found in a nearby alley. It was usually a teenager and always tied to gang violence.

One particular night when the shots were too close for comfort I once again called 9-1-1 and asked for an officer to come to our house. I pleaded with them not to park out front so they wouldn't arouse suspicion about who might be reporting crimes. The officer arrived thirty minutes later.

When the officer stepped into our house he took one look at me and all the kid toys lying around and asked, "What are you doing here?" I felt ashamed and sheepishly gave him our spiel of buying an investment property. We sat down at the kitchen table and he asked for something to write on.

I gave him a paper napkin and the officer drew a square in the middle of the napkin, "This is your house," he began. He drew a few lines indicating streets and alleys then made an X at the end of our street, "This area over here is controlled by the Bloods." He drew a second X at the other end of our street, "This area over here is controlled by the Crips. Your house is in the middle and these two gangs are using your alley to fight a turf war."

He continued explaining that the government subsidized housing behind our house was the first in the nation and designated a historical landmark. "It will never be torn down," he added. My first thought was how the real estate agent conveniently left that off her marketing materials.

Our outlook went from grim to hopeless. These were not isolated happenings but systematic and escalating gang wars. Not only were we participants in the economic mortgage lending meltdown, we were dangerously close to becoming a national homicide statistic. I shared this information with my ex wife the next day and once again we combed through our options.

It was around this time the economy began to falter and the real estate market started to decline. Even if we would have wanted to sell, it would have been difficult. If we did find a buyer, we would probably lose a lot of money. We felt like prisoners in our beautiful new home.

As the weeks and months passed I became desensitized and even cavalier to the sound of gunfire. It no longer startled me. My psyche had adjusted to the chronic stress. I was more afraid of a stray bullet penetrating our hardy board siding than of actual violence directed at us. I concluded that if someone wanted to do us harm they would have done it by now. We were soft targets. This blasé arrogance would be my undoing.

April 15, 2006 was a beautiful, sunny Saturday. It was one of those days you want to be outside and shake off the cobwebs of winter. My ex wife was on a women's retreat with friends and I was holding down the fort with the kids. It was a typical lazy Saturday.

Some time after lunch the girls were playing in the back room and I was in the kitchen. I heard the awful but familiar sound of rapid gunfire. The only disturbing aspect of it was to hear it during the day.

Following my familiar but morbid routine, I grabbed the phone and dialed 9-1-1. For reasons I cannot explain, what I did next nearly cost me my life. I went to the front door and stepped onto the front porch. I then became a witness to a violent drive-by shooting in progress at the end of our street.

Two cars were parked at the intersection in front of a house on the corner. After the last shot was fired the two cars sped away. One headed away from our house while the other came speeding in my direction.

I was distracted by the 9-1-1 operator asking me detailed questions and not paying full attention to the unfolding events. I was trying to be as helpful as possible by describing the make and model of the car. I then realized the situation was quickly turning from me witnessing a drive-by shooting in progress to possibly becoming a victim of a drive-by shooting.

Once I realized the danger, I stepped backwards inside the house. As I was backing away I saw a man's arm come out of the car window pointing a gun directly at me. I slammed the front door to escape the madness.

I remember commenting to the 9-1-1 operator, "Why is my house filled with smoke?" I then noticed light coming through the wall where light shouldn't be shining. I was not yet fully able to process what I was seeing. My eyes followed the trajectory from one wall to the other. What I saw changed my life forever.

I quickly realized I was now an active participant in a crime gone terribly wrong. In sheer terror I began screaming at the 9-1-1 operator who was becoming irritated but remained calm. I ran to find the girls playing in the backroom and while squeezing the phone between my cheek and shoulder I continued yelling at the 9-1-1 operator as I carried them upstairs.

I tossed them in a laundry basket and told them not to move and stay quiet. I shut the door and ran to my closet where I retrieved a 12 gauge shotgun my parents gave me when I was a young boy for hunting squirrels and rabbits. I quickly loaded it full of buckshot and waited.

Later I would learn that the car carrying the shooter pulled behind our house. I can only assume he wanted to find me in hopes of finishing the job he started.

In less than a minute the police had cordoned off our block. Our house was swarming with investigators, medical personnel, and uniformed police officers. They were supportive of my shocked state but also wanted to get as much information as quickly as possible.

I walked the investigator through my day up to the point when I heard the shots. I described how I walked to the door and onto the front porch and my realization that I was in danger. I described my quick, but not quick enough, backtracking into the house and slamming the door. It was at this point my story merged with reality and for the first time saw just how close I was to being hit by the bullet. A few feet away right at the level of my head and torso was a gaping, ragged hole in our living room wall. A little more panic and a little more shock settled in my body.

While recounting my story to the investigator an officer called out from the kitchen stopping everyone in their tracks, "I found the bullet!" Everyone turned toward the officer exiting the kitchen. She held one of my daughter's sippy cups with a bullet from a 9mm pistol inside.

This is the path the bullet took from the shooter's pistol to my child's sippy cup. After being fired from the car, the bullet penetrated the wooden railing on the front porch and passed through the front wall. After easily shredding through the wood railing and hardy board wall it tore through a layer of insulation and drywall. This is what exploded into a million little pieces filling my living room with what looked like a cloud of smoke. The bullet then exited the front wall passing through the opposite living room wall where it entered the kitchen cabinets and finally came to rest in my child's cup.

This tragic, mocking information was the final straw. Of all the places for a bullet to land, having it end up in something so innocent threw me into a state of shock. My body went numb. My mind went blank.

I thought it couldn't get any worse until it did. It was at this moment I received a call from my ex wife letting me know she was on her way home and only a few minutes away.

When she arrived I met her at the back door. In a moment of the worst possible timing she wanted to introduce me to her friend who wanted me to see her son for therapy. I didn't want to alarm her friend but there was still a real threat the shooter might be lurking somewhere nearby.

I rushed through an introduction then hurried inside the house. Once we were inside I could find no words to say. As we made our way into the living room my ex wife became disoriented by the mass of strangers wandering around. She looked at me then the officers looked at me. Everyone was waiting for me to deliver the horrible news. It was at that moment my ex wife saw the bullet hole in the wall. It took her a few dreadfully long seconds but finally she put the pieces together. The horror overwhelmed her. She collapsed on the floor wailing.

Rendering of the drawing made by a Nashville police officer explaining the gang situation

So What?

Why should this matter to you?

Ignoring the warning signs in your life doesn't just lead to regret—it can be deadly. If this story wakes you up to warning signs in your life that you have been ignoring, then it has done its job.

The truth is, I didn't just stumble into this dark, terrible situation—I walked right into it with my eyes wide shut. I kept choosing what I *wanted* over what was right and ignoring warning sign after warning sign. Eventually, the darkness almost swallowed me whole.

So what? Because we are all prone to ignoring what we don't want to see. We override our intuition. We silence our inner wisdom. We ignore the inner alarm bells because what we want feels so urgent, so important. But wanting something badly doesn't make it the right thing. And holding on to what's not meant for us can be more dangerous than letting it go.

This story matters because it's a mirror. Maybe you've been ignoring signs—nudges from God, concern from friends, your own gut. Maybe you're chasing something that deep down, you know isn't good for you. Maybe you're thinking the worst could never happen to you.

I did too and it nearly cost me everything.

One of the most sobering truths I had to face in this situation was that what happened to me was totally and absolutely preventable. I saw the red flags. I just didn't want to deal with them. And if tragedy had come for my children because of *my* recklessness, I know for a fact I would've never have been able to forgive myself or continue living.

If you're walking toward something you know in your bones isn't right—*turn around and run the other way!* If my life can be spared while sprinting in the wrong direction, so can yours.

This is your wake-up call. Don't irgnore it.

10

THE MIRACLE OF THE PEACOCK

The day my father died he was surrounded by his wife, his sister, and his daughter. I was 393 miles away in Nashville trying to thread the needle of seeing clients and taking care of the kids while wanting to be there with my father before he passed.

My father had been floating in a liminal state between life and death for several weeks following a fall and subsequent head injury. He was in a comatose state from the morphine and was not the least bit aware of his surroundings. It was unclear whether he had three hours, three days, or three weeks to live. He had always been dedicated to his work and I knew he would much rather me be working than sitting around waiting for him to die.

My mother was not alone but I wanted to be there for her during this difficult time. So when she called and told me he had taken a turn for the worse, I decided I should go soon. I would see a few more clients then leave for Mississippi. If I had known this would be the last day of my father's life, I would have left immediately.

After my first session I began to feel uneasy about my dad's situation. I was unsure what to do so on a whim I said a prayer asking my deceased grandparents (my father's parents) for guidance. I asked whether I should leave now or wait a few hours.

My grandparents were wonderful people. I remember being at their house all the time as a kid. There were always lots of cousins around, adventures to be had, and food to eat. I had the opportunity to live with them while in college and we grew even closer during that time.

I had no idea what kind of sign I was looking for or if this was how signs worked. I was desperate and needed some direction. I didn't have to worry because an answer arrived a short time later.

I was pacing around the house when I heard the familiar chime on my phone indicating a new email had arrived. I glanced at my lock screen and saw a notification from the Peacock Network (NBC). What I saw was an unmistakable message from my grandparents. But first let me explain why peacocks are so important to my grandparents.

My grandparents, and aunt who lived with them, were more like pioneers of the wild west than modern day people. They farmed their own fruits and vegetables and canned them for the coming winter months. They spent many summer afternoons on the front porch shucking corn and shelling pink-eyed purple hulled peas trying to escape the sweltering Mississippi heat. They grew sugar cane and operated a mule powered sorghum mill.

They once bought a big blue bus and traveled around the country in search of quartz, diamonds, and other rare gems. On these cross country excursions they did their fair share of panning for gold in mountain streams and rivers. My grandfather owned a gold plating machine and he would tumble the rocks they found until they were so shiny they looked wet. He then cut and polished them into ornate jewelry, making bolo ties and cuff links.

One day when I was about 10 years old I was following my grandpa around helping him with his morning chores. It was a chilly Saturday morning just after sunrise. As we walked out the back door we came across a very large black snake. Just behind its head was an abnormal sized bulge indicating the rascal had stolen an egg from the chicken coop. Without a second thought, my grandpa picked up the snake by its tail, twirling it around several times, then smacked its head against a tall pine tree, killing it instantly. Egg shrapnel splattered everywhere. I was both amazed and a little disturbed.

My grandmother, grandfather, and aunt were deeply religious people. If they weren't outside planting corn or inside cooking a meal for family and friends my grandmother and aunt could be found in the basement praying up a storm while my grandpa sat in his Barcalounger reading the Bible.

In addition to their various crops my grandparents raised dogs, cats, chickens, goats, ferrets, donkeys, and, yes, peacocks.

My grandparents *loved* their peacocks. They took their gorgeous feathers dappled with rich blues, greens, and yellows and decorated every room in their house. They had peacock art hanging on the walls and ceramic peacocks displayed in ornate glass shelves. This is why when I prayed for a sign and I immediately got a message from "Peacock" I knew it was a divinely timed message. What I saw on my phone was this: **Peacock. ENDING SOON. Don't miss this.**

I knew I had to leave immediately and kicked it into high gear. Within a matter of minutes I had canceled my remaining appointments, threw some clothes in a suitcase, and was on the road. After being on the road for only a few minutes I received a call from my distraught mother telling me my father had passed.

Screenshot of the day my father died showing a message sent from my grandparents about their son

Picture of my grandfather "Grandpa" (my father's father)

So What?

Why should this matter to you?

Sometimes what we call coincidence is actually communication. And if we're not paying attention, we'll miss it.

This isn't a story full of fireworks or headline-worthy miracles. It's quieter than that—more like a whisper than a shout. But it *was* an answer. I had asked a specific question in prayer—directly to my father's deceased parents—and the response came, not in words from the sky, but through a perfectly timed email notification containing symbols meaningful to me and my family.

So what? Because signs are easy to overlook. We would prefer it if God would communicate like thunder. But my experience is that we only get hints and clues through ordinary channels that have extraordinary timing. And it's the timing that makes it meaningful.

What strikes me is how uncomfortable people can be with the idea that our loved ones—those we were intimately connected to in life—might still be with us in some mysterious, spiritual way even though they have passed to the other side. Somehow, that idea is too out there for many, even though it's not just wishful thinking. It's biblical.

Jesus saw deceased people and knew things others didn't (John 1:48). His closest disciples saw Moses and Elijah alive and speaking with him centuries after their deaths (Matthew 17). Mary heard the voice of an archangel. Scripture talks about heavenly realms, councils, and spiritual warfare—all pointing to a multidimensional, active spiritual world (Psalm 82, Ephesians 6:12).

So what? Because as Christians we say we believe these things—and yet balk when the supernatural gets too personal, too specific, or too intimate. We believe God oversees galaxies, yet struggle to believe He might let a grandparent send a nudge to help their grandson make it to their son's deathbed before he dies. Why is that so hard to accept?

Here's the takeaway: If you ask God—or your ancestors—for a sign, be open to how the answer might come. Be willing to entertain the idea that heaven is closer than you think. Be humble enough to realize that maybe our modern skepticism is closing doors that God is trying to open.

Maybe the veil between this world and the next isn't as thick as we might think. Maybe love doesn't end with death. And maybe your next ordinary moment holds a message from somewhere (or someone) from beyond.

11

THE MIRACLE OF THE TRASHCAN

Even decent people do stupid things sometimes.

During the pandemic, I went a little crazy buying things I didn't need like extra bicycles, a generator, and a large freezer to store food in case the world came to an end. So I had a few extra items sitting around.

As time passed and the world returned to normal I used the freezer less and less. Food can easily get lost and forgotten after years in the bottom of a giant freezer. When it does finally see the light of day it is questionable whether it should be eaten.

My mother needed a freezer because she frequently entertains family and friends. That little freezer above her refrigerator just wasn't big enough. We were planning a trip to see her so I offered my freezer and she gladly accepted.

We were in a rush to leave so in an effort to get everything ready for the trip I pulled one of the large city issued industrial strength garbage cans from the alley up to my back porch. My son and I emptied the freezer so I could thaw it before transport. We didn't bag the food first, we just threw it in the garbage bin. In the back of my mind I had a nagging feeling this wasn't right and I should get a garbage bag. However, we were pressed for time so I brushed the thought away.

Early the next morning as I was taking my son to the bus stop I opened the garage door and sitting smack dab in front of my car was my large garbage can. It was blocking the way so I couldn't pull out.

That was strange, I thought, and got out of my car to put it back in its place next to the fence. That is when I saw a note taped to the lid. The note was firm and direct but not rude. It said something like, "The city will not take unbagged garbage. Please bag your food." The writer of the note left his name, Jim, and his phone number.

My heart sank. I knew I had made a mistake. I had not acted with integrity.

I opened the lid to the garbage can and was met with the foulest odor and tons of maggots! Oh, jeez! But I knew what I had to do.

I went inside and grabbed a garbage bag and a pair of blue latex gloves. I dove hands first into the nasty work of retrieving the putrid rotting food from the hot, moist depths of a filthy, foul-smelling garbage container. How did the food go so bad so fast? I knew this was my much deserved punishment for my laziness and poor decision.

Later that day as I was coming home I saw a guy putting a bag of trash in a can that I had never seen before. I knew without a doubt it was Jim.

I had a choice to make. I could ignore him and pull in my garage or I could roll down my window and apologize. I had no hard feelings toward Jim so I rolled down my window and asked, "Are you Jim?" He said he was and I apologized for what I had done admitting my fault.

Both of us had been living in houses that backed up to one another for years and this was the first time we had ever met. We ended up talking for forty-five minutes.

As we parted ways I thanked him again for calling me out. He accepted my apology and then seconds before leaving commented, "You might want to get that tree looked at," he said pointing to a nearby tree, "looks like a strong wind might take it down."

The forty foot tall tree had a gaping hole in the trunk eight feet tall and a foot or more wide exposing a nearly completely rotted core.

I couldn't believe it. For years I had walked by this tree when taking out the garbage but never had I really seen it. It was in terrible condition. What was worse, if and when it did fall, it would land on my garage, crushing my car.

Jim's parting words to me were, "Since it sits in the alley I think you can call the city and they might take it down for free." I thanked him again and knew that if I had to pay for this, which I would have to do if the city didn't, it would be a couple thousand dollars minimum.

That same day I called the city. They agreed to have someone come out and take a look. Days, then weeks passed and my anxiety grew with every howling wind and soaking rain storm.

Finally, an inspection crew arrived. They decided they could take it down and sprayed a bright orange dot on the truck signifying their approval. I was so relieved! Then more weeks passed and more howling winds tested the strength of that rotten trunk but no crew came to take it down.

After another month, I called the city. They informed me I was definitely on the list but there was a long backlog. I reminded them of the urgency of the matter and they promised to look into it.

Another month passed and my anxiety grew.

One day while on a run in a nearby neighborhood I saw a crew taking down a tree. I stopped and talked with them about my situation. They confirmed there was a backlog and said they would try to get to it soon.

That conversation must have sparked another conversation with the higher ups because in a matter of days a crew was in the alley working on the tree. Within a few hours the tree was gone. All that was left was a pile of sawdust. Not only did the crew remove the tree but they took my anxiety with it.

I took this situation to my *Sacred Space* time and reflected on how I had made a mistake, was called out, owned my mistake, and corrected my mistake. When I had a choice of coming face-to-face with my rightful accuser I chose kindness and humility over anger and embarrassment. Because I chose the high road I was rewarded with a decent interaction with a decent human being.

As an additional reward for subduing my ego, Jim probably saved me thousands upon thousands of dollars. Had the tree come down on my garage that in itself would have been thousands. Had it punctured through the garage and damaged my car, that would have been thousands of dollars and I would still have to pay for the tree to be removed! Insurance may have covered most of it but my insurance rates would have surely skyrocketed.

Some might think it is a stretch to call something so minor as this a miracle but to me it was most definitely a miracle on many levels. If I had not been trying my best to live with love, wisdom, and integrity I would have most likely responded to the neighbor's rightful complaint with either a bruised ego or just ignored him when I saw him in the alley. That is how I would have responded in the past. However, accepting ownership of my error in judgment allowed something beautiful to come from my mistake.

Hollowed out rotten tree in the alley behind house

So What?

Why should this matter to you?

Integrity isn't built in grand gestures—it's revealed in the small, seemingly forgettable moments. Like whether or not you take the extra 30 seconds to bag your garbage properly. It sounds trivial but it isn't.

This story isn't about trash—it's about character. About how easy it is to compromise when no one's watching, and how easy it is to justify it when we're rushed and impatient. So what? Because that's how people drift—one small compromise at a time.

I knew what I was doing was wrong. I felt it in my body. I had the thought: *Go get a bag.* But I didn't listen. I failed the test of integrity—not because I didn't know better, but because I chose convenience over conscience.

Then came the second chance. My neighbor Jim called me out—firmly, directly, but without a hard edge. So what? Because that moment gave me an opportunity: Would I double down in pride, or respond with humility? Thankfully, I chose humility. I owned the mess—literally and figuratively—and cleaned it up.

And here's the thing: this was a miracle of forgiveness. Not the flashy kind. The quiet, everyday kind. I had to forgive myself for falling short. Jim forgave me by handling the moment with grace. And in that confrontation, I noticed something deeper—a rotting tree. A metaphor, maybe. A reminder that the things we ignore—big or small—can decay if left unattended.

So what? Because people like Jim are rare, and we need more of them. People who tell the truth, who confront with kindness, who show us a better way of living. Jim didn't just correct me—he taught me. And now I carry that moment forward, so the next time I'm tested, I might choose better because of his example.

This isn't a story about garbage. It's a story about growth.

It's a reminder that your values aren't proven in big public declarations. They are revealed in the small, private moments. And sometimes, grace shows up not through divine thunder, but through a neighbor who tells you the truth

How you handle the small things is a big thing.

12

THE MIRACLE OF TIMING

On February 28, 2012 Penny Arévalo, staff writer for Patch.com, wrote the following article detailing the horrible and miraculous events of the day Kelli Groves and her two daughters were hit by an out of control truck driver high on methamphetamine. The driver died when his 18 wheeler barreled over the side of the bridge falling 50 feet and bursting into a ball of flames. The accident should have killed everyone but through a series of miraculous events 36 year old school teacher Kelli Groves and her two children survived. This article is printed here in its entirety with permission from Senior Managing Editor Autumn Johnson.

The Untold Story of a Crash that Made Headlines Around the World

The rescuers who pulled local teacher Kelli Groves out of a smashed car as it dangled from a Santa Barbara County bridge share their gripping recollections.

EDITOR'S NOTE: The dramatic rescue of teacher Kelli Groves and her two daughters as their car has drawn an outpouring of love and concern from local residents. Patch recently went to Buellton and sat down with one of Groves' rescuers – and talked with others by phone. It turns out, despite all the media coverage, some of the story has yet to be told.

As tow-truck driver Brian Gomez headed back to Santa Maria from a job in Santa Barbara on Jan. 12, he approached the bridge over Nojoqui Creek and saw what seemed like a movie scene: An 18-wheeler in the slow lane didn't follow the curve in the road; instead it crushed the BMW beside it, then went over the edge "like a snake going into a hole."

Next came an explosion 50 feet below. It sounded like a bomb, he said. Gomez slowed his flatbed truck so he wouldn't get caught in the aftermath and flipped on every hazard light he had. He called 911 and told dispatchers there wouldn't be any survivors. "There was lots of dust and smoke everywhere, pieces of truck everywhere," Gomez recalled.

Walking out on the bridge to survey the scene, the only reason he knew that the car hanging halfway over the guardrail was a BMW was because he saw it before the accident. Now it was completely unrecognizable. "It didn't look like anything, just a bundle of metal," Gomez said.

Approaching the carnage, Gomez's opinion didn't change: no survivors. "I thought there was nothing I could do," he said. Until he heard San Juan Capistrano resident and teacher Kelli Groves screaming for help. Gomez called 911 again to report there were survivors and to get ambulances right away. "Hurry, just hurry."

He rushed as close as he could to Groves. But the driver's side was suspended in midair. And there was no way to get Groves or her two daughters, 10-year-old Sage or 10-week-old Mylo, out. "Get us out of here," she told him. "My babies are in here. My kids are my life."

He tried to reassure her help was on the way. It would be OK. In the creek below, they could hear the big-rig's tires popping in the flames.

***

When the first calls came in, CHP Sgt. Donald Clotworthy, the on-duty supervisor that day, was in the Buellton station several miles away. He could see the smoke from his office.

Officers got to the scene quickly. Clotworthy said it did not look like a survivable crash. "No car is designed for impact with an 18-wheeler," he said. "We were very surprised that anyone was alive in the vehicle. … We were in awe that the car didn't follow the truck over the bridge. There's no's [sic] question there was luck or fate or something going on here."

Santa Barbara County firefighters from Buellton were not far behind. But a more specialized crew was only minutes away in Solvang. There, a group of experienced fire captains from around the county had gathered to become certified safety officers for incidents not unlike this one.

Six of them jumped in their engines and arrived far more quickly than they would have been able to normally, said County Fire Battalion Chief Woody Enos. He was one of them. Their efforts were split tending to the burning truck in the creek – investigators would later blame the crash on – and aiding the rescue above.

Enos said Kelli could feel the heat from the flames below. "The truck was burning literally right below her, and her feet were hanging outside of the car," he said.

Firefighters jumped in Gomez's tow truck but realized fairly quickly they weren't sure how to work it. So they asked Gomez to attach Groves' car to the winch. They also used ropes to secure the vehicle.

The car was basically twisted upon itself, Enos said. The rear passenger door was where the roof was supposed to be, the roof was on the driver's side, and the driver's side rear door was under the car. It was like a Rubik's cube.

When a firefighter tried to cut through the wreckage with the "jaws of life," the car would open up on the underside, where Kelli was trapped, her feet dangling ever more in the open air, Enos said. He called for a crane, but it would be awhile before one would arrive. "We were running out of options," Enos said.

What happened next has been widely reported. A group of Navy Seabees was traveling south back to its base in Port Hueneme in Ventura County. Stuck in the ensuing jam – traffic was stopped in both directions – the Seabees got out of their vehicles and asked how they could help.

Like the fire captains assembled in Solvang at the time of the accident, these Seabees were "the best of the best," said Clotworthy. They train other Seabees.

"What are the chances of that?"

More luck or fate or something.

"I talked to the fire captain in charge, and he was excited to hear that we had an extendable-boom forklift just 200 to 300 feet behind the wreck, and he said to go get it," said Construction Mechanic 2nd Class Michael McCracken in a press release the Navy published. Clotworthy had never seen such a forklift. "If I had to sketch out the kind of vehicle I would want, this is it," he said. "It looked like a Tonka toy a kid would play with."

With its low center of gravity and ability to extend the 10 feet needed to cross from the southbound bridge to just under Kelli's car, it was perfect, Clotworthy said. Gomez was more familiar with the forklift, having worked for construction-supply stores. He saw what the Seabees had to offer and thought, "We're golden." With that forklift, two firefighters could work the rescue, one to cut through the metal, another to assist Kelli and Mylo from the driver's side of the car, which still hung perilously over the creek, Enos said.

Daughter Sage came out first. As the gurney passed by Gomez, he noticed her doll fall to the ground. He grabbed it fast and caught up with her before she was placed in the helicopter. He would find out later that although she's not into dolls much, this one – a gift from her uncle named "Ruthie" – was really important. He would see her clutching it a week later as she prepared to leave Cottage Hospital in Santa

Barbara for the trip home.

Next was Mylo, and both Gomez and Clotworthy feared the worst. The baby hadn't been moving or making any noise the entire time. "I don't want to see this," Gomez thought. But then Mylo's eyes opened and her arms and legs started moving. She had a scratch on her forehead, but basically she was fine. (Clotworthy now believes Mylo had been asleep the whole time.) Gomez experienced a sense of relief he had never felt before.

"I wanted to cry," he said. "The other guys, they're professionals. This is what they do." Not Gomez. As a tow truck driver, he's usually called to a scene after a rescue. He's the cleanup guy. Removed from the situation.

Kelli was pulled out last. Unlike a movie, there was no applause. Just more sense of relief. Rescuers said they were really touched by Kelli's level-headed demeanor under the circumstances. "I think the true heroes are Kelli and Sage and Mylo," said Enos. Especially Kelli, the way she talked to Sage and kept her calm. "She deserves a lot of credit for keeping her family strong."

Everyone's kept in touch with the Groveses, emailing and visiting Kelli and Sage in the hospital and emailing more after they returned home. "Our heartfelt prayers and thoughts are with Kelli and Sage in their recovery," Clotworthy said. "We look forward to watching Mylo and Sage grow up. We've adopted them into our family."

Through her attorney, Kelli said: "The Groves family continues to look forward to personally thanking all of the rescue personnel and first responders to this unfortunate incident at the appropriate time after they are cleared to travel."

Kelli has been overflowing in gratitude toward him, Gomez said, but he's modest about his role. "I really don't know what I said. I don't know anything special I said to her," he said. All he could do was try to keep her calm while thinking the whole time that she could fall into the creek. "It was very heart wrenching, the whole thing. ... It was a very surreal thing. You wished it happened differently, but I'm so

glad Kelli and her family survived."

Clotworthy still marvels at the chain of good fortune – that Kelli's car landed where it did instead of going off the bridge, that a tow truck was immediately on the scene, that a crew of experienced firefighters from all over the county were within 5-6 miles, that passing Navy Seabees had the perfect tool to help the rescue, and that a car seat would cushion baby Mylo so well she slept through the event.

"As bad as the situation was, there were so many good things, remarkable things that happened. And it's without explanation," Clotworthy said. "We have to leave that for others."

The mangled car of Kelli Groves where she and her daughters were trapped

Kelli Groves car being supported by a special piece of equipment from Navy Seabees

So What?

So what? Why should this matter to you?

Sometimes life hands you something so wildly improbable, so full of beauty and divine orchestration, that it forces you to reconsider what's possible.

This story is packed with miracles—not small, easily-dismissed moments, but *big*, unmistakable interventions. The kind that, if you saw them in a movie, you'd roll your eyes and call it cheesy. Too much. Too convenient. Too sentimental.

And yet... *it happened.*

So what? Because this story forces us to wrestle with a question: What if God really does move in this way? What if the extravagant, the improbable, and the unbelievable aren't just the stuff of sacred texts or Hollywood films—but still show up in the here and now?

So what? Because the miraculous doesn't always fit neatly into our expectations. Sometimes, it doesn't look believable—not because it's false, but because we've grown so used to disappointment that we've forgotten how to recognize awe.

13

THE MIRACLE OF IMAGINATION

Ideas are the most powerful force in the world. Take love for example, it starts as an idea but so does hate. Ideas thought long enough become beliefs. Beliefs believed long enough become actions and what you do *is* who you are.

Not long ago I had a thought, an idea that seemed to come from somewhere other than my own mind. The strange idea was simple yet if I were to act on it, it would reshape my destiny like all actions do.

The idea was this: *It is time to live a more formal religious life.* As I reflected on this I assumed it was encouragement from God given its spiritual context. What was odd about the timing of this idea was that I had not been to church in more than five years.

In 2003 my now ex wife and I returned to Nashville from Seattle, Washington where I was in graduate school. We felt the desire to reestablish ourselves in a church for both social connection and spiritual guidance. Our former church had changed over the years we lived in Seattle and it no longer felt like our community. After some discussion, we decided to try something new.

Many of our friends attended St. Bartholomew's Episcopal Church. Neither my ex wife nor I had ever attended a "high church". High church refers to a service that follows a strict order with lots of standing, kneeling, and communal prayers. Many Episcopal churches get labeled as the "frozen chosen" for this reason due to their lack of emotion during the services.

We loved St. Bartholomews from the moment we entered the sanctuary. As we made our way to the pews we appreciated the myriad of stained glass windows and high arched wooden ceiling that resembled what Noah's Ark might have looked like from the inside. It was then we noticed beautiful music coming from somewhere we could not see. There were no musicians on stage as is typical for many churches especially in Nashville where Grammy winning artists are as common as high fives at Bonnaroo. We turned to search the back of the church and up in the loft hidden out of sight were the musicians, pipe organ, and choir. We appreciated that the worship was not a performance.

From 2003 to 2019 our family attended St. Bartholomews. We created many wonderful memories from christenings to Christmas pageants. Then in 2019 a series of unfortunate events began to unfold that left my ex wife and I feeling disconnected from ourselves, each other, and our St. Bartholomew's community.

By early 2020 our divorce was in full swing. The Episcopal church had a schism over gay clergy. The longtime priest we adored retired and the global killing machine known as the COVID-19 pandemic was just getting started. It felt appropriate to hit the pause button on everything. For me, that pause button lasted more than five years. During that time I maintained an active spiritual life; it just didn't look like it had in the past.

Divorce has a way of making you reevaluate your entire life including what you believe about God. Instead of going to church I had a powerful healing psilocybin experience in the mountains of California. I studied Kabbalah for a year with a teacher from the Los Angeles center. I explored astrology with a wonderful lady out of South Africa. I met with a psychic who connected me with my deceased grandfather. And every Sunday I preferred cleaning my house instead of going to church. It was in the midst of five years of this when I received the message that it was time to live a more formal religious life.

At first I was confused by the directive. I did not understand what the message meant in a practical sense. However, believing it was a message from God I took it to heart and got to work solving the riddle and exploring my options.

After a five year hiatus, I returned to St. Bartholomew's and it felt like home. I was greeted with open arms by old friends and new. I had heard good things about the priest, Father Josh, and set up a time to meet with him.

I began to meet with him regularly and soon the assistant priest reached out to ask if I cared to join a men's group she was organizing. My first reaction, as is always my first reaction with social events, was to say thank you but no thank you. However, remembering my injunction to live a more formal religious life, I decided to entertain the possibility. It took me a while to warm up to the idea but I eventually accepted the invitation and joined the group. The priest eventually asked me to be the convener (leader). Episcopalians have a lot of strange words for normal things.

During this time I went on a spiritual retreat to Saint Meinrad's Archabbey Monastery. It was there I had the wonderful experience of meeting Father Eugene which I describe in *The Miracle of Joy* chapter. This jump-started my interest in becoming an Oblate which culminated with my investiture ceremony at St. Meinrad's surrounded by monks in March 2025.

In one of my meetings with Father Josh he asked me if I had ever considered becoming a LEM. I told him I didn't know what a LEM was or did. LEM's are lay eucharistic ministers he said. During each service, Father Josh consecrates the bread and the wine then distributes the bread/body of Christ at the communion rail to the communicates saying, "The body of Christ. The bread of heaven." The LEM's follow behind him with a silver chalice full of consecrated wine/blood serving the communicates saying, "The blood of Christ. The cup of salvation". Being openhearted about whatever experiences were coming my way I agreed to become a LEM as well. After committing to being a LEM I had the most fascinating dream.

The dream begins with me walking into some kind of bar-like establishment. It was at night so it was dark outside but it was also dark inside like a club. There were lots of good looking young people milling around, black lights making things glow, and a casual chill vibe. For a musical representation of what the bar felt like search on your preferred music platform for the *Simulation Swarm* by Big Thief or *Spitting Off the Edge of the World* by Yeah, Yeah, Yeahs ft. Perfume Genius.

Out of the blue a lovely young lady came up to me and started waving her hands up and down in front of my face saying, "You have clean lines." She then walked away. I was confused and had no idea what she meant.

A few minutes later this same young lady came back with another young lady and the first lady started explaining something about my "clean lines" to the second lady. It was clear the first lady was trying to teach the second lady something.

After the two ladies left I noticed other people staring at me and whispering to one another as if I were on display. I felt a little awkward the way any old guy might feel in a bar full of young people gawking at him.

Then a beautiful young man came up to me. He had golden blonde hair swooped over to the side like a surfer and the brightest blue eyes that sparkled. His smile was captivating. It wasn't a big toothy grin. He smiled with his eyes. It was full of wonder and amazement.

As he looked at me with an intense ferocity he started speaking to me in a language I did not understand. It could have been Latin. He then smiled at me and reached out to touch me. The moment he made contact with me a jolt of electricity filled my entire body. It was so powerful it caused me to convulse so violently that I woke myself up bouncing on my bed, panting and out of breath.

I had no idea what had just happened. I looked at the clock. It was 3:00 AM. I laid back down trying to sleep but that wasn't happening. There was too much adrenaline coursing through my body. I did what most people in my situation might do and reached for my phone to check my email.

I was not scheduled to serve as a LEM for a few months due to the rotations already being scheduled. However, as I scrolled through my emails I saw one from the LEM group thread. One of the LEM's was sick and needed a last minute replacement. I quickly responded that I was available.

My first time serving as a LEM was beautiful. I had a wonderful experience and felt deep joy serving the congregation in this way. On the drive home I remembered my dream and suddenly realized that the young people in my dream were angels! As I reflected on my dream further, I realized the bright blue eyed young man was Jesus! He was empowering me to serve the wine/his blood to the children of God.

As my conversations with Father Josh continued, our discussions slowly turned toward what it might look like for me to go through the discernment process to become a priest.

It was during this time that I engaged in a writing experiment where I imagined Jesus talking to me and answering my questions. This experience happened spontaneously. I did not sit down with my journal and contrive the idea to converse with Jesus. I just wrote a question at the top of the page and a conversation ensued.

Over the course of a few days I wrote ninety-six pages. I would love to believe these conversations were supernaturally inspired because that is what they felt like while I was writing them but an argument could be made that they were more imagination than miracle. Either way, what happened allowed me to feel closer to and connected with Jesus in a deeper, more intimate way.

Using one's imagination to connect with God has precedence as a practice in the spiritual life. The Jesuits call it *Imaginative Contemplation*,

> *Imaginative contemplation is all about getting to know Jesus. It is a method of prayer in which you imagine yourself as present in a Gospel scene, stepping into the story and encountering Jesus there. It was St Ignatius' firm belief that God can speak to you just as clearly in your imagination as through your thoughts. This way of praying will help you to see more clearly, love more dearly, and follow more nearly the person of Jesus Christ.*

I have included the full transcript of my conversation with Jesus. It is embarrassing in places and reveals maybe too much personal information but a writer writes and this is what I wrote. Hopefully, you will find some of these conversations inspiring and deepen your own dialogue with Jesus. It is always a good thing to move deeper into your spiritual life whether that be through service to others, writing, other forms of art, or long walks in the woods. Jesus wants to connect with you in whatever way you most understand.

As a note, my words are in normal font. Jesus' words are *italicized.*

FIRST CONVERSATION WITH JESUS

Jesus, what do I do to solve my money problem?

I will provide.

Thank you!

I will provide, Reb.

I trust you.

I will provide.

I believe you.

Have I not given you blessings to overflowing?

Yes. You have.

Worry not. Sin not. Love more. Be joyful. Trust in me. I will not let you down. If I did I wouldn't be who I said I was.

Where does my power come from?

Who says you have power? Your power comes from your humility not your strength.

I want to ask, what do I do?

Ask anything you want.

But I feel like you're going to say, "Be, first."

Money is energy. Prayers are energy. Sex is energy. Love is energy. Thoughts are energy. Learn to be an energy tamer like David Blaine kissing the snake. Learn the secrets of money.

OH NO! This is starting to sound like a church special series/infomercial/cult!

I don't mean secret secrets, just ways of money that might not be commonly known or understood.

Can you share one of these secrets with me now?

Yes. Money belongs to you. Take it. A certain amount of money belongs to you and no more. Take what is yours. Leave the rest for others.

How do I know how much is mine?

If it flows to you, it's yours. If you have to wrestle for it or it doesn't flow to you, it is not yours. Go where the money flows to you.

Thank you!

You're welcome.

SECOND CONVERSATION

Ask a question to get things started. What do you want to know, really?

Will you help me with the question?

Of course. Be still and listen. Follow me, Reb. Create on earth what is in heaven.

Ok.

What are you feeling?

Nervous. Anxious. Fearful.

Give those to me.

Ok.

You are storing up treasures in heaven. Keep going. You can trust what you feel, Reb. Trained, disciplined emotions with integrity are gifts from God.

Thank you.

You're welcome. Trust does not mean do what you feel all the time. It just means there is something true in your emotions that can be trusted. Reb, you are pure of heart. Wear that as a badge of honor. Let it be more and more true each day.

I will and I have a question. Is this communication with you real or my imagination?

Both are true. How else would I speak to you if not your imagination, a burning bush?

Well, I would most likely be more convinced that way.

Yes, probably. I love you, Reb.

I love you.

I just spoke with a real estate broker. It felt okay. I don't know if I am truly trusting you or trying to will myself to trust you. How will I know the difference?

Do you "try" to love your girlfriend?

No.

Right. It is natural, effortless, right? Just trust. Clean up your mind. Ask me anything you want any time. I am always here for you to give you what I want for you, what is good for you. You Abba Father is a good gift giver.

Yes. Amen. Hallelujah.

The answers you seek are so close. Keep looking.

Why do I have to "keep looking"? Why can't you give them to me?

There is a lesson in the journey that is part of the story. It is good. You wouldn't want to miss it. Remember how good the sunglasses experience felt?

I do.

Magnify that times 10,000.

Oh my.

Yes, oh my. I love that you keep telling people the sunglasses story.

I love that story. It is a miracle.

Yes.

THIRD CONVERSATION

Will I win the scratch offs?

Now we are getting somewhere! Yes. No. Maybe.

What does *that* mean?

There are some parts of your story you cannot know in advance. There is a plan and part of that plan is learning to trust me more. When you begin to doubt and lose faith, say, "I trust you".

I believe in miracles. How can I bring more of them into my life?

By listening. Listen to God. Listen to life. Listen deeply to other people. Miracles are everywhere. You cannot arrange things outside of space and time but you can be a kind ear to someone hurting or bring joy to someone on their birthday. Those may not seem miraculous to you. They may seem small. But often the love with which the gift is given is the miracle. What may seem small to you means a tremendous amount to someone else.

How can I know the will of God?

You will know it is the will of God by its fruit. If it produces love, joy, hope, courage, happiness, peace, kindness, it was from God.

I've always wanted to know the will of God before I act but you're saying I will know it after?

Nothing you think is black and white. There are times when you can know beforehand the will of God if that is good and right. It is a gift from God or as you like to say, "a miracle". It's both before and after.

Am I doing the right work?

It is the right work but not in the right way.

What is the right way?

The right way is what works to bring the most good, with the most love, to the most people.

Again, thank you.

Again, you're welcome.

I don't know what I should ask. What do you want me to know?

Just talk to me. You can ask anything.

Ok but I would hate to have Jesus on the line and not make the most of our time.

Who of you by worrying . . . the next few years are going to be hard for everyone.

What do you mean?

America made the choice to walk a hard path. That was the free will choice of the nation. Like individuals, countries have a freewill. The word for America is destroy. It will be heartbreaking to witness. Prepare yourself as much as possible then lead with love, wisdom, and integrity. Americans will be in great need of these virtues. Don't forget faith and hope. Remember, bring the most good, with the most love, to the most people. Where others destroy, you rebuild. Where others choose hate, you choose love. When others are foolish, you choose wisdom. When others are deceitful, you have integrity.

What are other things you would like us earthbound souls to know?

You are not alone. You are never alone. Call out every hour of your life for help, guidance, assistance, support, miracles, love, wealth, any good thing. The more you ask the more you receive. Be patient with each other. You are only human. Your imagination is a gift from God, a direct line to heaven. Use it. Visualize what you want. It will attune your spirit to opportunities in the physical world.

Ok. I think I'll take a break but please interrupt me if you need to say something. I am so grateful for this way to communicate.

FOURTH CONVERSATION

How was your day, Jesus?

Lovely. Thank you for asking.

Do you get overwhelmed by all that goes on in the world?

No, not in the way humans get overwhelmed. There are two big differences between where I am and where you are. I see everything all at once. But more importantly I know my father's plan because He showed me. It's magnificent. It is probably better said I get impatient on your behalf. I want you to see Abba Father's plan. You are hampered by the veil. You see things not as they are but as they are behind the veil. You cannot see them in their fullness. Your inability to see fully breaks my heart. But one day . . .

FIFTH CONVERSATION

Good Morning Jesus. I just finished my morning prayers. I am so concerned about finances that I can hardly think of anything else. How do I trust you more in this area?

God be with you, Reb, you are putting forth such good effort. That is your job right now, to lean completely on me, trust fully in me. The fear you feel is when you fall back on thinking you have to do it all. Trust me. Remember what I told you to do?

I trust you, Lord

I trust you, Jesus

I trust you, God

I trust you, Spirit

I put all my trust in you knowing you will guide my steps and put words in my mouth. I trust you, Jesus, help me trust you more!

I am praying for you now, Reb. I bring your concerns before God, your Abba Father, and the Holy Counselor on your behalf. I pray for a breakthrough for you in the earthly realm where abundance flows freely to you. I ask this in my Father's name for you. Now receive all the blessings that are yours.

Hold open your hands to symbolically receive the gifts, your gifts, from your Heavenly Abba Father.

Write down these words, Reb. Pay close attention throughout each day. Each hour holds a mystery and a gift. Your work is to find the mystery and receive the gift. Your Father loves you and desires your heart to be happy.

Thank you.

Gladly. Do this every day. Every hour of every day until this season of giving is over. It will be a while until it is over. Any gift you find will be yours. You must have eyes to see and ears to hear. Ask for this dispensation. It is your birthright. These are the gifts set aside for your life. God loves you. Receive freely. Walk in faith. Use each gift for the most good, with the most love, to the most people.

It is my desire to do as you say. May it be as you say, Jesus, son of the living God. Amen!

As sure as the sunrise, God will bless you. Nothing can stop God's love for you. Everything that happens is for you. God wishes for you to know his closeness as you have never known before. You have only tasted a cup of water. He wants to give you the ocean. May it be so.

May it be so! You have shown me miracles, signs, and wonders. Thank you.

You are so very welcome, Reb. I love you.

I am happy being with you. Thank you.

I receive your happiness. I will store it in heaven with the Father and the Spirit forever.

Will you help me write a book?

Yes.

Wow. A book by Jesus.

It is a book by you. I am only the inspiration. You write. I inspire.

There is a block within you, Reb, from being truly, wholly free. You are hesitant to step into the freedom you have been given. Your reluctance will only slow the flow of gifts coming your way. This is not wrong or bad or a sin. It is a water hydrant turned slightly on rather than full blast. Imagine the water slowly dripping. Put your cup underneath it. Watch it slowly fill. It is still life-giving water. But how much more quickly will the cup fill to overflowing so much that it splashes everywhere, watering the ground beneath to bring forth life. Even the blessings that fall to the ground will bring forth life. Open wide the hydrant so that it floods the world!

May it be as you say, Jesus! I love you!

I love you. Now use your imagination and open the hydrant. It never stops, Reb, never. Good work. I love your imagination. "Every step you take. Every move you make. Every single day. I'll be watching you."

That's fun.

Let this be our song, Reb.

You got it! Pretty intimate.

My love for you knows no bounds.

I love this.

Every hour of every day I am with you. I am with you.

Every day I pray. Every day I say. I am with you. I love you.

Now we are connected in Spirit and in Truth. When you drift away, always come back to me. I am here for you always. We can go as deep as you wish.

I receive that invitation for the most good with the most love to the most people.

I know you want to talk about money. It is always okay to talk about anything with me, Reb, anything any time. I am here for you.

Well, now it doesn't feel like I need to talk about it any more!

Good! Go on a run in the rain then.

Ok.

SIXTH CONVERSATION

I see now why you wanted me to run in the rain! You wanted to link the vision I had in my imagination with the spigot opening and seeing the neighborhood flooded as a metaphor to the reality of seeing the streets of my neighborhood literally flooded with water. How brilliant and playful! Thank you.

You are surely welcome.

So can anyone do what we are doing? Can anyone reading this have this kind of closeness I am experiencing?

Anyone. Anywhere. Any time. Remember, my mission on earth is for the most good, with the most love, to the most people.

Wow. Just wow. When I was away from the tablet I thought I heard you say, "It's time to go full spiritual". Did you say that or did I make that up?

It is always time for everyone to go "full spiritual". But I understand what you are asking. It is time for you personally to dedicate yourself to spiritual endeavors.

Yes. But I also hear what you are saying. We all need to be more spiritual all the time so the answer is always yes.

Take in the statement in its simplicity and let it transform your life.

I will.

Spiritual connection is very much tied to physical health. The body is one of the greatest miracles in all the universe. You are tired now having exercised. I know how much you want to keep our connection going but you need to rest. It is okay. I'm not going anywhere. Take a break. Your signal needs recharging so you can receive my thoughts to you. Exercise is perfection but don't forget what you put in your body impacts your spiritual health. Eat better. Exercise more. Drink less alcohol though I would prefer none. I know you are human. Too much alcohol completely blocks the ability to spiritually connect leaving you open to attack by the Enemy. That is actually the worst part of alcohol. If you are going to drink, you should pray before, during, and after. All your defenses fall like sand castles in the rising tide of alcohol. Be careful.

Thank you for noticing my tiredness. I do want to push through and connect but I should pause.

SEVENTH CONVERSATION

Pray every hour for your miracle to be shown to you so you can see the power of God at work. Prayer every hour of every day. Here is a simple prayer for you to say, "Abba Father, May the miracles you have stored up for me in heaven be used down here on earth for the most good, with the most love, to the most people."

That is a beautiful prayer. I want to ask questions about my father, about sex, about heaven.

As Father Josh said, "All sin has consequences." This is very important to remember even if the effects are not felt in the moment. Sin is turning away from what is good to do what is evil. There is always a turning away moment with sin. That moment when you choose to do what you know is not best. When it comes to any behavior that you are not sure is right or wrong, invite me into the moment. In a sense, I am already there but your invitation is for me to take action rather than just witness. Your invitation to me turns sin on its head. That is what I came to earth to do, to turn sin upside down so you can be free. Always always always invite me into your life at every turn. There is no place I won't walk with you. Let the Spirit always hover over your life.

I know John 3:16, the world's most famous Bible verse, tells us why you came so I don't think I need to discuss that. But what about a message for our time?

The messages from God are always the same generation to generation. But because each generation must relearn the same message it bears repeating. One of the most important lessons for your generation right now is that everything you do matters. Every action, every thought, every word uttered has either a consequence or a benefit. They get logged in the infinite book of God. That is what is so important for this generation. So many people fall into two types of darkness. They either feel entitled to do whatever they want, whenever they want, to whoever they want or they go to the other extreme and feel like they don't matter at all to anyone and nothing they do matters. These are dark places.

When people start to understand that they matter, their life matters, their actions matter, they have started down the path of wisdom. It is really just a change of perspective that is all it takes yet that small shift is a miracle of epic proportions.

Seek always to trust me. Ask for what you want. Do what is right and no matter what unfolds, the best path will open in front of you. Be faithful and watch for miracles.

Ok. I can do that.

EIGHTH CONVERSATION

I am concerned about my work.

We have talked about this already. Trust me. Say, "I trust you".

I trust you.

You know in the past I have deeply hurt people I care about and because of that I have so much regret. Will I ever be able to move past this? How do I move past hurting those I love?

Again, all sin has consequences. This hurts my heart for you. The ramifications make the Enemy happy. That was his intention the whole time. He was setting you up little by little until you stepped into the trap. Once you did, the deed was done and you could never go back. This is the pattern the Enemy uses with everyone.

The Enemy is here to steal, kill, and destroy. No one can undo what they have done in the past and must live with the consequences. Praise Almighty God you have turned away from your sin and sought repentance. You were offered the keys to the kingdom with the great and powerful gifts of love, wisdom, and integrity. You have made them the core of who you are and how you work and it has been counted to you as a blessed miracle. You chose well and continue to choose well. This is your path to full spirituality and away from sin. Sin doesn't mess up my connection to you. It messes up your connection to me. Think of sin like dark storm clouds blocking the sun. The sun is still there doing its thing.

I can hardly believe this is possible, that I am spending time with Jesus and I am drawing a blank on what to talk about! All my life I have wanted to talk to you and here it is. I wasn't prepared. This is really a miracle. I don't want to do anything else.

I think I would be remiss if I didn't ask about evil.

What do you want to know about evil?

Nothing right now. I'm sorry I asked.

Do not worry. Ask anything you want.

I just don't want to have a flippant, morbid curiosity about evil.

Yes. Stay away. You are correct, evil has a wicked little voice.

NINTH CONVERSATION

Good Morning Jesus. I pray for our conversion today to be filled with joy, love, and wisdom. Amen. What is it like where you are?

Miracles are common here. They grow on trees like fruit. Everyone works hard to bring their loved ones these gifts. Everyone is also about the work of the Father. We all want the beauty and love here to be on earth as it is in heaven. This is home. It feels like home.

Can we talk again about how to know the will of God?

While miracles are all around, it takes a leap of faith to trust that what you feel, see, and think are in line with the will of God. You cannot escape the necessity of trust when life does not look like how you want it to look. Trust is love. Love is trust. Go through every day trusting God and you will go through every day loving God. This is the will of your Abba Father.

My mind seems so preoccupied with money that every time I am still, my mind returns to that subject.

Do as you wish, Reb. God can and will take everything and make it good. You cannot fathom how much power is in the simple word "good". To take anything and make it good is the true act of good. No one can do that but God. God only wants your good. Therefore, God wants what is good for you.

Pray this, "God show me what is good in your sight. Keep me from sin. Help me love your children. Thank you."

I love to talk about what is good. It is what powers the angels to do their work. The angels only sing of what is good. There is no power greater than good because all good things come directly from the heart of God. This goes for what is good in heaven and what is good on earth.

Take a good joke that doesn't demean another person. God loves comedians. He loves to see his children laugh. Laughter is good for the soul. Heaven is full of laughter.

How can I love my girlfriend better?

Accept her just as she is right where she is. She is a force that will not be easily moved. This was the lesson she needed to learn from her marriage, to stand strong in her convictions.

Laugh with her. I love that you call her your Joybringer. What a beautiful name. That is her spiritual name. You two have a special love.

Thank you! Thank you! Thank you for her!

It is our pleasure, truly. You have both been through a lot. In the best possible way you two deserve each other. To answer your question about how to love her better, ask me this question every day, "How can I best love my girlfriend today?" Then listen throughout the day and I will show you.

I will.

Good.

Your writing is art, Reb. Think of it that way. Many people will find great comfort in these words. Because you listened to me they will realize they can listen to me and see how easy it is to connect with me. I love to spend time this way with you. I know you are loving this too. You love words and ideas. Those are the currency of love in heaven. Good ideas come down like rain nourishing the hearts and minds of those in tune with God. All words you send to heaven are precious in the sight of God. All words.

What do I do about my children's lack of spiritual lives?

Love them. Love is their spiritual language. It does not look like you but it will one day. Love them and pray for them. You cannot imagine the power of the prayers of a father. It is beyond your words to understand how powerful. A mother's love and prayers already have a special connection to their children. But a man needs to create that connection. Your love and prayers will build their faith. Pray always for every aspect of their lives. Do not worry but pray instead for them. They can stand on the shoulders of your faith. That is the power of a father's prayers. As a father, you will either create faith for them or destroy faith. Always love them. Always pray for them. Always build their faith. That is your job. The rest is between them and me. All will be well as you pray for them. As you pray for your children you get to see directly into the heart of God and what God wants for you and how God sees you.

Can you say more about praying for miracles every hour?

Anything that pulls your attention toward God is worthwhile and beneficial. Prayer is often deeply misunderstood and because of this confusion, it is not practiced as often as it can be and therefore the power of the faithful is less than it could be. Think of prayer like charging your phone or your car up to twenty percent. You could only use it for as long as the charge lasts then you would need to charge again to use it. It is the same with prayer. It charges your soul making it more powerful. You can't begin to comprehend what prayers from those on earth do in the heavenly realms. It powers those in heaven whether that be the angels or your ancestors. Everyone benefits from prayer. So make it a habit at the top of every hour to pray.

I have heard that we choose a lot of our destiny before we come to earth like who we will marry, our enemies, and we have these soul contracts with people to learn lessons. Is that true?

The primary purpose of a soul's existence is to choose to love the Father with all of your being. Heaven is a lot like earth life in the sense that heavenly beings do things. They are productive. They create. They share their gifts with others. There is no soul on earth by accident. It was a choice. The purpose, however, is not to learn lessons but to love God. One of the ways souls can love God is by ascending to greater heights and depths of spiritual awakening. The way people do that on earth is by learning lessons from mistakes or making intentional efforts to sacrifice in order to learn a new skill or serve others. So yes, it is true that earth life is a choice and souls do learn lessons while there and things are arranged in a sense but it is not for the gratification of the soul. It is to bring honor to God's grand plan.

If someone wanted to do what I am doing with you how would they go about that?

Grab a pen and some paper and start writing! This experience you are having is a grace extended to you. Had you asked for it, it would not have been given to you. The grace was extended because you were ready for it. You have been putting a lot of effort into your spiritual life and it felt like it was the right time for this experience for you. That is why you were given the grace not because you asked for it. You cannot earn this grace. So whoever reads these words can relax. There is no formula you can do to create this experience. Having said that, the Spirit meets all who seek Her. I know you have questions about that pronoun. We will come back to that.

Why I continually say pray every hour is because doing so along with other spiritual activities make your spirit ready to receive gifts such as this. So everyone who listens to the Spirit may not get this gift but they will get a gift that will help them on their journey.

Okay, back to my "Her" comment. I love that you often ask the question, "Where is the feminine in the trinity?" It's right here in the Spirit. It is so glaringly obvious but when I came to earth it was a male dominated world so the nature of the Spirit had to be obfuscated in order for the message to be received. Now things are better for women but theologians get so tied in knots about the language that they cannot allow the idea of a feminine part of the trinity to exist in the language. Patriarchy is still a real thing as well and men want power and with the backing of theologians they ignore the female/feminine. It is there. It will always be there. The Father is different than the Son which is different than the Spirit.

The reason we created man and woman was to reflect God's nature of feminine and masculine and it is also why we allowed humans to create and have babies to reflect the Son. Everything on earth is a reflection of a Truth in heaven. Let me say this clearly, not honoring the feminine is dishonoring to God and dishonoring God is another way of saying sin.

TENTH CONVERSATION

The line is quiet, Jesus. I want to connect but nothing is coming. Up until now it felt so natural, effortless. I don't know if this is over but the connection is not here at the moment. I will wait a little longer then go do something else if it doesn't light back up. I do feel somewhat off. Not sure what it is I feel. I had the idea to write a Thank You note.

(Later that day)

Dear Jesus,

These last few days connecting with you have been unlike anything I have ever experienced. I am forever grateful for this special time with you.

I must admit I felt . . . what's the word . . . unprepared. How could I be at a loss for questions to ask Jesus!? I just feel a little silly now. That's all.

I know this was a grace you gave me not because I earned it but because you wanted us to have time together because you love me.

Maybe the point isn't that I have good questions to ask you to get information but just to be with you. Asking questions is how we get to know each other. Being together is the point, not learning new information.

I just can't help but think that if I asked the right questions you would share with me things that could change the world then I get a bunch of people to follow my work like that *Conversations with God* guy and I sell a lot of books and never have to worry about money again and I have something to pass on to my children! Gross!

But that is how part of me feels. I want to help a lot of people and I want to make a lot of money. Can these go together and not be gross? I don't know.

The reality is you have already done what needs to be done and said what needs to be said. I can't add to that.

Whatever happens next I will cherish this time as exceptionally special. Thank you for our time together. It was/is dear to me.

Finally, thank you for never giving up on me when I was blind and lost and didn't even know it. I was walking around asleep in a coma acting as if I was awake.

I love you Jesus and I know you can search my heart and know that is true. That makes me happy and that brings me peace.

I Love You,

Reb

ELEVENTH CONVERSATION (Ten Days After Last Communication)

Jesus, can this continue to happen, these conversations between you and I?

Yes. You can ask me anything, Reb. Everyone is deserving of miracles because everyone is made in God's image. I like your idea of writing things down you want to ask me. I feel your hesitation, your doubt. It is normal. Keep your mind clear and focused away from distractions.

I like that.

Good.

What was up with my emotional heaviness earlier today?

You were under attack brought on by your excessive alcohol use the night before.

What was the attack about?

The Enemy is trying to stop your progress. Your power is increasing daily. You are getting stronger. Because the Enemy cannot stop you, it is trying to slow you down with doubt, fear, and anxiety. Your excessive alcohol use allowed an opening for the Enemy to get a foothold and torment you all day. It was good that you reached out to others. You regained your balance by not drinking tonight and asking for my help.

TWELFTH CONVERSATION (17 Days After First Conversation)

Good morning Jesus. Just checking in.

Good morning, Reb.

I have been so deeply moved by the Holy Week services.

Yes. Me too.

You haven't been writing down ideas to talk about. Why not?

I'm not sure. Laziness?

Whatever you want to know. Whatever you want to ask. We are united. Let me know. I am here.

Thank you.

You're welcome. I sense your hesitation. Give your hesitation and doubt to me.

Ok. I love you.

I love you too.

I trust you.

Yes. You do.

Help me today.

I will.

Is there anything else you would like me to know today?

Wait on the Lord and all will be revealed.

Amen.

Trust me, Reb.

I put my trust and faith in you, Jesus. Show me the way.

Walk in love, wisdom, and integrity. Look for me everywhere you go.

I will do as you say.

Abundance is the word, Reb. Focus on that word. This is what I give.

I receive your abundance in all ways.

God the Father loves you, Reb.

I receive God's love. I crave practical help. Can you give me something practical?

My peace I give you. My peace I leave with you.

Thank you. I love you.

Jesus, I am getting more comfortable with this way of communicating with you.

Good.

I want to become bolder when I come to you to be completely open and free.

Yes!

Help me live the story you want me to live.

Trust in the Lord with all your heart and lean not on your own understanding. In all your ways acknowledge Him.

Show me where to go and what to do please.

I will. One step at a time.

Thank you.

Of course.

When you don't know what to do, Reb, live fully in the present moment you find yourself. That will lead you to what is next. That is the simplest way to live life. Act when you know what to do. Be fully in the present moment when you don't.

Thank you. Help me be present and know when to act.

I will. Be. Act. Be. Act. Be. Act. Be until you know what to do. Act until you no longer know what to do. Then be again.

This is powerful.

Yes. While you are being, remember to be in prayer.

Is there anything else before I leave?

Play around with your power, Reb. Get comfortable with it. Read at church. That will take you out of your comfort zone. Feel the energy of being in front. You need to practice this.

Lose weight. You have become too comfortable at times which is being reflected in your drinking and weight gain. Be healthy in all areas of life. Fast more often and you will experience two gifts. One from me and one for your health.

Anything else?

Again, pray before, during, and after you drink. Together we will walk through what is healthy. I want to be invited into all areas of your life.

I don't have any more questions now but I know I will.

Write them down!

Yes. I will. This feels like a good place to pause.

Very well then. Have a beautiful day, Reb.

Okay. Thank you.

You are so very welcome.

Here are some highlights from my conversation with Jesus:

- *You can trust what you feel. Trained, disciplined emotions with integrity are gifts from God. Trust does not mean do what you feel all the time. It just means there is something true in them that can be trusted.*
- *Just trust. Clean up your mind. Ask me anything you want any time. I am always here for you to give you what I want for you, what is good for you. You Abba Father is a good gift giver.*
- *When you begin to doubt and lose faith, say, "I trust you."*
- *The right way is what works to bring the most good, with the most love, to the most people.*
- *You are never alone. Call out every hour of your life for help, guidance, assistance, support, miracles, love, wealth, any good thing. The more you ask the more you receive. Be patient with each other. You are only human. Your imagination is a gift from God, a direct line to heaven. Use it. Visualize what you want. It will attune your spirit to opportunities in the physical world.*

- *The fear you feel is when you fall back on thinking you have to do it all. Trust me.*
- *Pay close attention throughout each day. Each hour holds a mystery and a gift. Your work is to find the mystery and receive the gift. Your Father loves you and desires your heart to be happy.*
- *Exercise is perfection but don't forget what you put in your body impacts your spiritual health. Eat better. Exercise more. Drink less alcohol though I would prefer none. I know you are human. Too much alcohol completely blocks the ability to spiritually connect leaving you open to attack by the Enemy. That is actually the worst part of alcohol. If you are going to drink, you should pray before, during, and after. All your defenses fall like sand castles in the rising tide of alcohol. Be careful.*
- *Pray every hour for your miracle to be shown to you so you can see the power of God at work. Prayer every hour of every day. Here is a simple prayer for you to say, "Abba Father, May the miracles you have stored up for me in heaven be used down here on earth for the most good, with the most love, to the most people."*
- *When it comes to any behavior that you are not sure is right or wrong, invite me into the moment. In a sense, I am already there but your invitation is for me to take action rather than just witness. Your invitation to me turns sin on its head. That is what I came to earth to do, to turn sin upside down so you can be free. Always always always invite me into your life at every turn. There is no place I won't walk with you. Let the Spirit always hover over your life.*
- *So many people fall into two types of darkness. They either feel entitled to do whatever they want, whenever they want, to whoever they want or they go to the other extreme and feel like they don't matter at all to anyone and nothing they do matters. These are dark places. When people start to understand that they matter, their life matters, their actions matter, they have started down the path of wisdom. It is really just a change of perspective that is all it takes yet that small shift is a miracle of epic proportions.*

- *Seek always to trust me. Ask for what you want. Do what is right and no matter what unfolds, the best path will open in front of you. Be faithful and watch for miracles.*
- *Sin doesn't mess up my connection to you. It messes up your connection to me. Think of sin like dark storm clouds blocking the sun. The sun is still there doing its thing.*
- *Go through every day trusting God and you will go through every day loving God. This is the will of your Abba Father.*
- *You cannot fathom how much power is in the simple word "good". To take anything and make it good is the true act of good. No one can do that but God. God only wants your good. Therefore, God wants what is good for you. Pray this, "God show me what is good in your sight. Keep me from sin. Help me love your children. Thank you."*
- *You cannot imagine the power of the prayers of a father. It is beyond your words to understand how powerful. A mother's love and prayers already have a special connection to their children. But a man needs to create that connection. Your love and prayers will build their faith. Pray always for every aspect of their lives. Do not worry but pray instead for them. They can stand on the shoulders of your faith. That is the power of a father's prayers. As a father, you will either create faith for them or destroy faith. Always love them. Always pray for them. Always build their faith. That is your job. The rest is between them and me.*
- *Everyone who listens to the Spirit will get a gift that will help them on their journey.*
- *Let me say this clearly, not honoring the feminine is dishonoring to God and dishonoring God is another way of saying sin.*
- *The Enemy is trying to stop your progress. Your power is increasing daily. You are getting stronger. Because the Enemy cannot stop you, it is trying to slow you down with doubt, fear, and anxiety. Your excessive alcohol use allowed an opening for the Enemy to get a foothold and torment you all day.*

- *When you don't know what to do, live fully in the present moment you find yourself. That will lead you to what is next. That is the simplest way to live life. Act when you know what to do. Be fully in the present moment when you don't.*

Investiture ceremony by monks of St. Meinrad's Archabbey

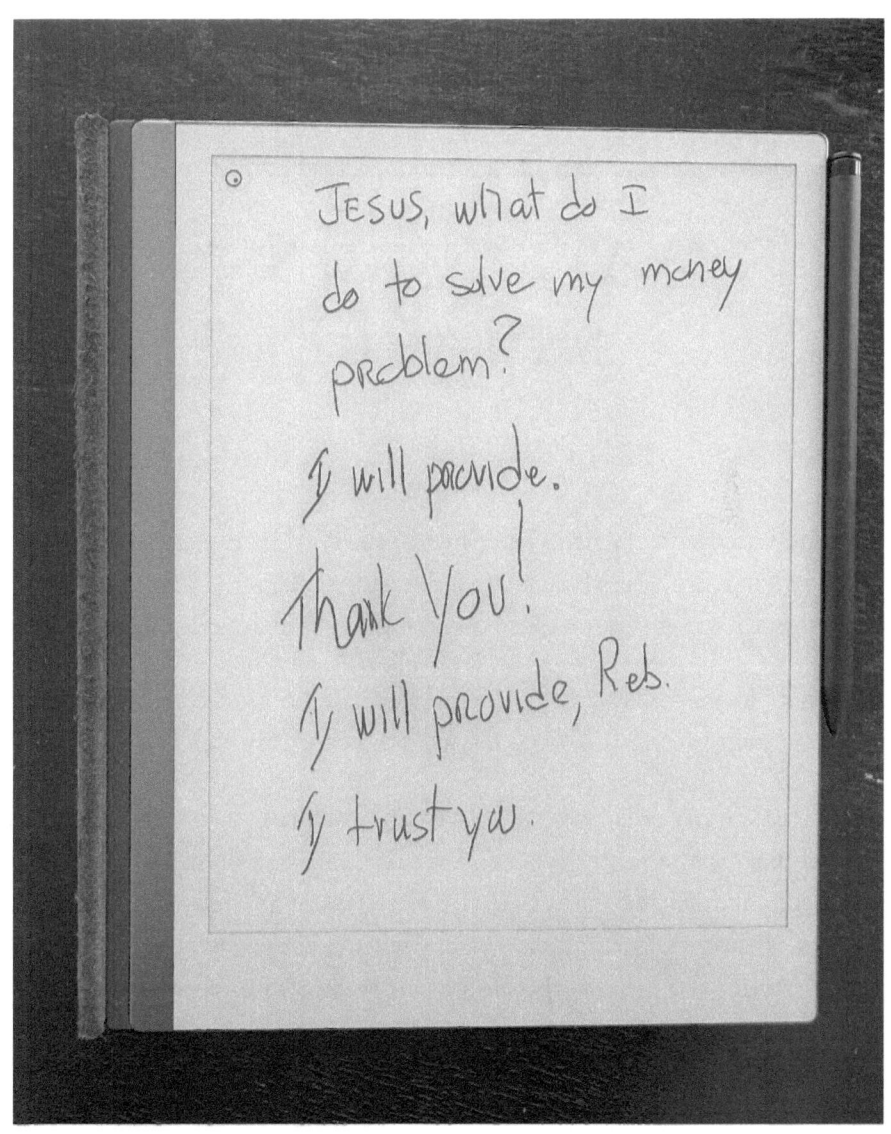

This is the first page of 96 pages I wrote in my Remarkable tablet of my conversation with Jesus

14
WAITING ON A MIRACLE

The vast majority of my life has been lived in the silent gaps between miracles. Miracles may be more frequent than most of us realize but I still don't see them nearly as often as I would like.

So what do we do when we have tried all we know and prayed as much as possible yet the miracles we need don't arrive?

The most courageous act of faith we can practice is believing that this, too, is part of the plan. Even as I write those words my body wants to reject them. It leaves us begging the questions, how can a sincere person faithful to God quick to ask for forgiveness who seeks an authentic relationship with the God of all creation not receive a miracle in a time of need? The only answer that makes any sense is that there is something bigger going on we cannot see or understand.

If there is a map for our lives we are blind to it most of the time which leaves us wandering around confused without explanation or understanding of the terrible things that happen to us.

As I write in my prayer **Be Still - A Prayer To A Silent God**, *"And when I do ask for what I think I want or need, my prayers often go unan-*

swered. This leads me to conclude that either I am far adrift from your divine will for my life or your silence is essential to our relationship."

In this disoriented state of silent unanswered prayers, our job is to do everything we can to keep our hearts open. A closed heart, even if it is closed for legitimate reasons, interferes with the signal from the Spirit. An open heart is the most hopeful response but it is hard to hold onto when fear is hunting us down seeking to steal our peace.

There might not be a more heartbreaking space for an earthbound soul to occupy than sitting in the silence of God when a miracle is needed. Our mind goes to crazy places. First, we turn on ourselves believing we must be the problem. We analyze every word, every action, every thought in hopes of rooting out our great sin that has caused God to hide his face from us. We convince ourselves that if we can earn our way back into the good graces of God our miracles will come.

When we have exhausted all the dark corners of our own heart and mind but no miracle arrives we turn our dark thoughts on God, lashing out in hateful sorrow. *How could you allow this to happen? Why do I believe in you if you don't show up when I need you? My friends and family are right, faith is a fantasy for people who can't cope with reality. If you really loved me like you say you do, you would help me.*

Take a deep breath. Seriously, take another deep breath. It's okay. Now you know the truth of what is buried deep within your heart. It may not be pretty but it is real. Turning doubt, fear, and anger over to God may be all there is to do in the absence of a miracle. You can hold onto them if you want but that is a painful and lonely way to live.

Pray. Wait. Listen. Trust. Hope. Love. Surrender. Repeat.

I believe in miracles because I have experienced miracles. I believe with all my being that you, too, can experience miracles. One of those miracles was the Spirit's instructions for me to live every day with love, wisdom, and integrity. Whether your miracle has arrived, you are still waiting on a miracle, or you are waiting for your next miracle, you can always return to love, wisdom, and integrity as a guide for how to live your life. This way of living will make you more sensitive to the miracles all around you.

15

PRAYING FOR A MIRACLE

People looking for miracles are in dire need of something that will solve an urgent, and often serious, problem. Unfortunately, there is no formulaic step-by-step process anyone can follow to manifest miracles on demand. The best way to spiritually align with the mysterious realm of miracles is, in fact, the same way anyone needs to live to be a good Christian and decent human being.

I can only speak from a Christian perspective because I have little in-depth knowledge of other religions. However, the Bible has much to say about how one should live.

In the Book of Proverbs it tells us to trust God with all our heart and do not depend on what we think we know. In the Book of Mark it tells us to love God with all our heart, soul, mind, and strength. In the Book of Romans it tells us to be transformed by the renewing of our minds. In the Book of Ephesians it says be kind and forgiving. These and many other verses call us to live a virtuous and noble life.

Here are fifteen ways to pray for miracles in your time of need. Some of these require great discipline and courage and are not for the faint of heart.

- Pray for what you want and for God's will to be done
- Pray for a miracle
- Pray until you get an answer
- Pray every hour of every day as you go about your work
- Pray at night until you go to sleep
- Pray for angels, saints, and ancestors to intercede for you
- Pray for more faith and trust in God
- Pray for miracles for others in need
- Pray for an open heart to receive the miracle
- Pray for your faith to grow from unanswered prayers
- When your miracle arrives, share the story with others
- When a miracle arrives celebrate it
- When a miracle fails to arrive for you or someone else, mourn together
- Pray for courage to accept the outcome as the will of God if the miracle doesn't arrive in time
- Do your very best at some point every day to get still physically, mentally, and spiritually then be quiet and listen

We have come a long way together. When we started I prayed a blessing for you and as we end I want to leave you with a blessing. It is the mantra I say over myself everyday. I invite you to borrow it until you come up with one of your own:

May you be loving today

May you seek wisdom today

May you act with integrity today

May you have a courageous heart today

REB BUXTON, M.A., O.S.B.

Reb received his B.S. degree in Banking and Finance from The University of Southern Mississippi in 1994. He worked in accounting for years at Vanderbilt University and later the entertainment management company Flood, Bumstead, McCready & McCarthy.

Reb attended The Seattle School of Theology & Psychology in Seattle, Washington where he received his Masters in Psychology in 2003. He has worked in the mental health field as a case manager, counselor, and center director before starting his private practice in 2014.

Reb has worked with couples all over the world to help them bring more love into their relationships by strengthening and deepening their connection to one another. He is on a mission to bring more love into the world one client at a time and one marriage at time.

Reb has spent the past year receiving spiritual direction training with the monks of St. Meinrad's Archabbey Monastery. His investiture ceremony to join the monastery will be held in February 2026.

Reb has written three books *The Hard Work of Happiness, Listen - Connecting To Your Intuitive Wisdom,* and *SUPERNATURAL - Evidence For Miracles In Everyday Life.* He is currently working on his fourth book about living from inspiration.